Stock Investing for Beginners

The Most Comprehensive Guide to Learn the Definitive Investment Rules & Strategies for Passive Income and Achieve your Financial Freedom

Jack Copson

Table of Contents

Investing in Index Funds

Index funds are another great passive investment. They provide investors with the opportunity to gain exposure to the stock market without trading in individual stocks. This is an important feature as it helps diversify risk. On the whole, index funds give investors exposure to an entire stock index, that is, a whole array of stocks. As a result, this diversification mitigates risk. This is the ultimate way of putting your eggs in various baskets.

Getting Started With Index Funds

The first step is to select the right fund for you. There are several funds. So, it's important to review them all before setting your sights on one.

Here is a list of the major ones:

The Wilshire 5000

The Russell 2000

The NASDAQ Composite

MSCI EAFE (mostly European and Asian stocks) The Dow Jones

There are also other smaller stock indices. The smaller ones tend to be custom-made products set up by financial corporations or hedge funds. They are pitched to individual investors or may represent a specific niche. You can look into these if you are keen on investing in a smaller fund. However, these funds may require higher investment capital. So, it's important to keep that in mind.

Index funds are pegged to a specific stock index. For instance, Dow Jones groups the 30 largest companies in the United States. In comparison, the Wilshire 5000 is based on the 5000 largest corporations. This implies that there is a much broader selection of companies.

Making Money With Index Funds

Buying into an index fund can be done in one of two ways. The first way is through an online platform, such as in the case of day trading. In this case, you select your fund and buy into it. Depending on the fund, the minimum

The amount of investment capital will vary. In some cases, you can buy into the fund with as little as $200 or $300. With these funds, you'll find that they offer moderate returns. Roughly speaking, index funds perform at the market average. On the whole, you can expect a run-of-the-mill fund to perform at around 6% a year.

That's much better than the returns you'd get on a regular high-yield investment account.

Thus, you make money as long as the market is up. If the market experiences a downturn, as you would expect to from time to time, then you may end up losing money. This is why index funds offer good value as they are invested across a wide range of companies and industries. Unlike industry-specific ETFs, index funds look to spread out your asset allocation as much as possible. This is how you can achieve these returns.

All About Fees

It should be noted that index funds come with fees attached. These fees are generally charged for account maintenance. This is true of funds that human money managers manage. Naturally, the institution issuing the fund needs to cover overhead. If you are keen on having a human money manager handle the fund, this would be the best option.

However, there are index funds that are managed by Robo-advisers or trading algorithms. As such, they don't require any human interaction. These funds offer a great deal of value as they charge minimal maintenance fees. In some cases, they don't charge any fees at all. So, it's worth looking into an index fund managed by a Robo-advisor. Often, automated fund managers beat average market returns. So, this bodes well for you.

Setting Up Your Strategy

When you go about setting up your strategy, there are two possibilities.

The first is the "buy and hold" strategy. This is a long-term strategy that you can use if you aren't in a rush to make significant returns. This approach is highly passive and capitalizes on the snowball effect. In short, the longer you leave your investment intact, the more money you make. Also, you can simply roll over your investment every time the interest payout comes

Around. If your fund offers monthly payouts, then simply roll them over. If interest payments are quarterly, you might consider pulling a portion of it and rolling over the rest.

The great thing about the buy-and-hold strategy is that it doesn't take a lot to get started. You can begin with whatever the account minimum happens to be. Then, you can add more funds to the account as you can. Over time, you'll see your investment begin to take off.

The second approach is a much more aggressive one. In this approach, you open up your account with the minimum required. Then, you commit to putting as much as you can into the fund. However, you are not looking to buy and hold for the long haul. When you choose to take a more aggressive approach, you need to be ready to pull your money when the market is heading toward a recession. As a yardstick, the stock market enters "correction" territory when it's down at least 20% from its previous high.

Taking 20% is not a good investment. Consequently, you need to be ready to pull your investment as soon as you see trouble ahead.

To facilitate your chances of pulling out ahead of time, you need to make sure that there are no time restrictions. Some funds may ask you to keep your money invested for a certain time frame. If this is the case, you might be on the hook for a few months or even a few years. If the markets take a downturn during that time, you have no choice but to go along for the ride.

However, if you have the freedom to pull your money as soon as trouble looms, you can do so freely. Then, you can reinvest once the crisis is over.

As you can see, index funds are a great way to enter a passive investment without having to make a significant upfront investment.

Investing in Private Equity

When we refer to private equity, we're talking about taking an ownership stake in a private company. This means that you are not buying stock from a company that's traded on the stock market. Rather, you are investing in individual companies such as startups.

Investing in private equity generally involves funding a new company or providing startup capital. In most cases, this requires a significant investment, often thousands of dollars. Now, it's important to note that private equity means that you receive shares, or a stake, in a company in exchange for your cash.

So, let's take a look at how you can make money by investing in private equity.

Taking Part in Crowdfunding

Entrepreneurs turn to crowdfund when they need capital. This capital can be used for any number of aspects related to the business. Since finding individual investors that can provide them with capital is hard, some entrepreneurs turn to crowdfund.

In these crowdfunding campaigns, entrepreneurs usually offer incentives to their investors. For instance, they'll offer limited-edition products. In other cases, entrepreneurs may choose to issue stock in exchange for funds. These are the types of opportunities you can take advantage of.

During some crowdfunding campaigns, entrepreneurs may put up a few thousand shares at a specific share price. Depending on the price, you can buy up a bunch of them. In other cases, shares may be so cheap that you can buy up a decent lot for a couple of hundred dollars.

Making money in this type of approach is rather straightforward. You can hold on to the stock until the company begins to expand and take off. At that point, you might get a buy-back offer from the founders of the company. At that point, you can sell for a profit. Otherwise, you can sell to other investors later on.

Taking Dividends

If you choose to hold on to the stock, you should be eligible to take dividends. Dividends are the portion of the profits that shareholders are entitled to. Since you were generous enough to invest your money in a given company, you should get a cut of the proceeds.

However, you need to be careful. Please ensure that the terms and conditions of the stock issue state that you are eligible for dividends. This is important to note, as the terms may state that you would be eligible for dividends after a specific time frame. Therefore, you need to be aware of this before pledging your money.

Still, taking dividends can be a great way of adding another revenue stream, especially if you aren't in a hurry to see a significant return on your investment.

Scoring on an IPO

Some startups take off to the point where they choose to go public. When a private company goes public, an event known as an Initial Public Offering (IPO) takes place. A fixed share price is set based on the number of outstanding shares and their valuation during an IPO. If you were fortunate enough to get into this company before it took off, chances have you scored shares at a very low price. By the time the company is ready to go public, shares would be worth a lot more.

The way you make money here is by selling your stake once the company has gone public. However, you need to do your homework. Investors who sell right at the opening of the IPO may end up missing out on massive profits.

Generally speaking, companies soar in the days following the IPO. In that event, you could make a killing.

However, not all companies soar following their IPO. Some pullback before taking off. So, the safe bet is to sell right at the start of the IPO. This is the most effective way of ensuring a good return. This is the ultimate buy-and-hold strategy for private equity.

Cashing in on a Takeover

There are cases in which larger firms take over private companies. When this occurs, shareholders are bought out entirely. In general, the founders retain some interest in the company (it's usually a token gesture), while the rest receive their fair share.

Much like an IPO, when a private firm is bought up, it is valued based on its financials and earning potential. This valuation is then divided by the number of outstanding shares. It's at this point where investors clean up. There are cases in which the larger corporation may be willing to pay a premium on top of the share price as a means of getting the deal done.

The Key Is to Get in Early

Most startups do several rounds of financing. In the early going, crowdfunding is one of the easiest ways in which entrepreneurs can raise capital. It can be very hard to attract venture capital firms in the early days. So, smaller investors may find a good opportunity to make a significant investment. Thus, the key to making money in private equity is to get in early.

The caveat here is to make sure you avoid sinking in too much money into a single company. This is important as most companies don't pan out over the long-term. In some cases, you'll get your investment back. In the worst of cases, you'll miss out. Most of the time, you'll make a modest profit.

So, it's important to keep in mind that private equity is about holding your stake for an extended time frame. It might be a matter of years before you see a significant return. But if you happen to hit a home run, it will be worth the while.

There are three things to look at when you plan on investing in private equity:

1.   The market for the products and services of the company

2.   Sales projections for at least five years

3.   The company's track record

If a company fails to produce any of these three items, pass on it. Any company you plan to invest in should at least produce some kind of track record that can back up their claims. Otherwise, investing in an untested company may be nothing more than wishful thinking.

The Anatomy Of Dividend Investing

The holy grail of investing has been searching for and achieving a reasonable return rate on one's assets. This may be a struggle to neutralize risk at a reasonable yield despite relatively low-interest rates and a wide variety of investment options.

While not as trendy as a hedge fund or "exciting" as selling options, investing in companies paying rising dividends is a solid foundation for anchoring the investments. We assume that the cornerstone of the investments will be high-quality dividend stocks. Why? Why?

1)   Research has shown that such payout securities are reliably cheaper in the long run than other securities. Approximately 30 percent of cumulative portfolio returns are made from dividend payers.

2)   Throughout the years, they have a growing influx of revenue. Each year, that's a salary raise!

3)   We also sell mere growth stocks in today's competitive markets to cover verse rates.

4)   We put together four main points to help you grasp the highest performing businesses' structure for dividends. You will be able to find, pick, and extend your dividend portfolio by following these criteria.

The Root Of The Matter-Dividend Growth

The lifeblood of dividend income is dividend development. Inconsistency may be a symptom of a problem, much as in the heart rate. The same refers to transactions in payout securities.

The cohesiveness of the dividend increase is the main factor. While the same figure will rise year after year, it is more critical to be raised by a constant number every year. Our rule of thumb is to search at businesses with an annual 5-7 year growth of 7-10 percent. Instead, after it, the organization offers you a pay boost per year. It was lucky that our employer lifted 2-3 percent-especially in this environment, to most of us.

The Muscles Vs. Fat The Payoff Ratio

It appears like Hanz and Franz, but note, weight is still significant. This can have its benefits (so that you can show off your "muscled" body, with facial expressions shouting "Pump [clap} you up"). Why? Why? When required, the body turns fats into sugars to provide strength. If you like, a contingency

Fund. The same refers to dividend distributions. Sure, just not at the cost of comprehensive employment. You want money. Put specifically, the distribution ratio is the number of dividend profits. For example, a business receives $2 and gets a dividend of $1, and it has a 50 percent payout ratio.

By understanding the firm's dividend payment ratio, you can stop purchasing stocks whose profit is too small, and most specifically, unsustainable.

Which is to be avoided?

- 75% or higher tier

- 30% or a smaller amount

- Inconsistent compensation rates

Buying such securities typically contributes to a lower yield, accompanied by reduced product costs and, finally, a buyer's remorse.

We tend to identify businesses with a profit level between 40% and 60%-the perfect spot. This offers the owners a good return while maintaining enough capital to fund expenses, grow the company, and increasing the dividend (pumping up the earnings).

A Strong Business

Well, it's about dividends development, as dumb as this can sound. Not a hot new inventory or drug. While you want to invest money, this approach is more about the return, year after year. The third critical point, since contemplating an enterprise's dividend growth strategy and distribution ratio, is the company's coherence across the economic cycle. This is where "fad" goods and services and businesses "dying" try to be stopped. Buggy whips, CB radios, and Pogo sticks were not checked despite being revolutionary and famous in their day. Boring is a positive thing here. I like to see businesses that will market their goods ten years from now at better rates irrespective of the economic cycle.

Don't Sell The Stocks.

Even because stuff often doesn't fit in a personal partnership. And yes, it can be challenging to break up, but generally, it turns out to be the right thing. The same goes for owning a stock.

It's all right to "like" your inventory, but don't fall in love with it. Emotion and money do not destroy your spirit, but your pocket certainly does crack. Learn the signals that things are shifting. Earnings, for example, are that (one

A missing quarter is ok), but not an overall structural improvement.

Often the economy offers you the chance to earn faster than you expected. Although we are not in favor of selling, it is prudent to remove some of the benefits off the table if the stock has significantly risen in a limited time (say 40 percent in six months).

The same is accurate at the edges. When a stock declines 20%, and the basics are still fine, adding more to the fund is smart. But, if things get wrong with the firm's sector, sell your place and search for other opportunities. As our parents claimed, there's a lot of fish just in the water.

While not as comprehensive as Grey's Anatomy, our anatomical dividend investment framework would encourage you to diagnose your portfolio informally. The aim is to draw on a plan, the methods, and the practice. This is the best thing about the business; it still offers chances for buying or selling.

Buybacks Or Dividends: Which Are Good For Shareholders?

Savings and equity buybacks are commonly used as a means for a company, as practical counterparts, to "return the money" to its shareholders. However, they are not at all equivalent.

Indeed, the only link between dividends and equity buys is that the corporation requires a part of its profits to pay for it. When you are a client, it is the capital that the company controls. The Critical Stock Investor should not be oblivious to the mechanism by which it uses to return its shareholders' money. See what the gaps are and determine for the Rational Equity Investor what is better.

Dividends are straightforward: the corporation sends you the money. Dividends are always declared quarterly, approved by the Board of Directors, and forwarded a few weeks later to the shareholders. The Board claims that the payout is $1.00 per vote. They send you $100 if you have 100 shares. What would be more straightforward?

Share buybacks are often not complicated, nor more than dividends. In the case of stock repurchase programs, the Board permits the company's retained earnings to buy shares of the company on the open market. The plan may be that, for example, the company would buy 1,000,000 shares in itself in the next six months and take them in and out of the market. If the stock during the plan sells an average of $20 per share, the company pays $20,000,000 to purchase its shares.

Why are these two very different actions, often referred to as similar ways of "giving money" to shareholders? In principle, the company uses part of its remaining profits to transfer the interest to its owners. With dividends, capital itself is "something of value." The organization will give you a report. The "something of value" comes with the buyback of the share in the form of an increase in each market share value. When the company buys X shares, the remaining (theoretically) shares are worth more to its holders. The corporate cake has been divided into smaller and, therefore, marginally larger pieces. The cumulative number of outstanding shares reduces, meaning that each remaining stock is a higher percentage of the company, a slightly higher yield on its potential profits.

All right, say you're a business owner. Will you be worried about the direction the organization uses to give you "any value?"

Here are the benefits and the reverses of the dividends:

•   Pro: They are the right money in your wallet. It's all for the abstract. You can invest that money in the company again or do anything you want. You can use it as revenue.

•   Pro: Most dividend programs are corporate policy equivalents. Companies never slash or delete dividends. While each dividend payout is a different case, the overall scheme is sacrosanct at most businesses paying dividends.

•   Pro: Dividends help support a higher share price, provided a substantial dividend program worth on the market. Research demonstrates that the market puts interest on dividend schemes over long stretches.

•   Dividends are closely monitored and reported, so it is easy to get information. Over time, companies establish pretty predictable dividend patterns. Critical trend shifts are recorded immediately.

•   Con: You have to pay dividend taxes. However, the 15 percent federal income tax limit on distributions makes it one of the least taxable income sources available.

Below are the advantages and drawbacks of share purchases:o pro: Because you don't get money, you are not taxable.

•   Pro/con: The repurchase of shares decreases the number of shares available and increases the remaining stock's worth. To understand this improved interest, however, the company needs to update the remaining shares.

You are abstract only if and when this occurs.

•   Con: You're not sent any money. When you want the value of the capital, you have to sell any of your shares. The income you receive from the sale is then charged at the rate of capital gains, either on a long or short-term basis (as long as the transaction is more costly than the shares you initially paid). The long-term government limit is 15%, the same as for distributions. The short-term limit is the most likely higher marginal tax rate.

•　　　Con: Stock repurchase schemes of most companies are "one-offs" and not healthy. Scale or size are not reliable.

•　　　Con: Stock buyback schemes are not closely supervised. Most of them are never done until their first release. Inconsistently, these errors are published in the financial press.

•　　　Con: Most businesses buy back shares and repay their executives (and other staff) on equity incentive awards. The executives turn around and promptly refund the shares to the company as they are included in their pay plan. Therefore, the equity buybacks of the corporation are insurance expenses for the client. The managers, not the owners, get the money.

•　　　Con: Stock repurchases are always made at the lowest share price. The initiative should be rolled out in reaction to a surge of income, which contributed to a higher share price in the market. That may also be that the corporation now wants the shares to pay for decisions that the corporation can not manage.

Unfortunately, management works in many companies that profit more than shareholders, although the shareholders are the company's owners. How is this happening? For a big, multinational corporation - whose fiduciary responsibility is to protect the owners' long-term interests - the Board of Directors is also hostage to management. Management proposes, and the Board does not carry out its supervisory function effectively. It comes at the center of too many financial controversies over the past decade.

Compare that with a private corporation. Many of these corporations may be very broad, but their ownership is not so different from that of a publicly-owned corporation. In such a company, the company works for its founders- who often sit on the board. The Management Council is not in isolation, and management is a slave of the Council as it needs to be. For these businesses, you assume that significant dividend distributions are part of the package for the founders. Dividends remain well ahead of sales, as business earnings say. Whatever income is not required to finance ongoing activities or extension is directly passed to the sellers. When you are the sole owner of a business, wouldn't you?

Therefore, if one of the financial goals is current profits, dividends will now be more attractive than equity repurchases. They come regularly (and are often increased); they come in cash format, which is income at once; they are taxed at a low rate, and they do not require you to sell shares to realize what "valuations" are transferred to you. Moreover, the fact that management retains a robust payout policy shows that the business is run for its owners' well-being rather than by command. The administration is expected to make wiser decisions on remaining earnings (after payment of dividends), which will favor you as a long-term investor.

Dividend Stocks Outlook Yield High

The Federal Reserve has stated that it plans to hold historically low-interest rates for a long time, and inflation looks to be under pressure. The results in the first quarter will turn up well in contrast to anemic estimates in the end. Retail revenues seem to be returning when we exit the slump. Unemployment has declined and may also marginally decrease. The aggregate economy has been recovering significantly since the lower months, and large sums of cash are also on the brink of coming back into the business.

On the other hand, our national debt has risen to an alarming pace with introducing the stimulus program at a terrifying rate. Middle Eastern geopolitical instability also remains crucial as we are now in two conflicts and have ongoing nuclear issues with Iran. While Al-Qaeda is searching for new safe areas to meet in Syria, we see growing problems. Global warming problems remain unanswered. The world's ambitions to come to some collective consensus, as demonstrated by the "non-results" of the Copenhagen meeting on dealing with it. Our Government is also worried that too much debt would jeopardize our ability to continue paying loans by exporting treasury bills to India, Japan, and other foreign front countries. Interestingly, we consider a second stimulus package to ensure that we do not slip into stagnation, given these fears. In general, the crystal ball our economists look into the future can be a bit more blurry than average because what is going to happen is tough to foresee.

And what does that mean for stocks with high yield dividends? It's still lovely, as they say, to predict the best and plan the worst case. If 2019, with low-interest rates and an improving economy, turns out to be a continuation of the last three quarters of 2017, we will see the whole industry expand faster, and the stable yield on dividend stocks will raise their values right away. This is more important because we reflect on the other case: what if it goes the other direction and 2019, for economic or geopolitical purposes, or a mixture of both turned out to be a downer. Then what happens to stocks with big dividends? Suppose you are early in your investing career and are seeking to develop a retirement portfolio. In that case, a downturn in the market offers you the opportunity to purchase quality stocks at a bargain price.

This is especially relevant if you implement a dollar-cost averaging system (regularly buying a certain dollar sum from a given stock or product) and have high yields on securities and reinvest dividends. When you invest monthly, the cheaper your inventory, the more shares you purchase every month, and the dividend would maximize the annual return relative to a non-dividend paid growth stock. On the continuum opposite end, you tend to collect the earnings stream as you withdraw and survive on dividends from your investments and keep high-quality dividend return securities irrespective of whether the price has increased or deteriorated. Compare this to an investment plan focused on using a percentage of non-dividend paid income securities in an investment fund. Based on a forecast annual growth rate of 8%, it appeared appropriate to deduct 4% of sales each year.

The problem is that optimistic growth forecasts in the real world do not always come true. If the market declined again in 2019, removing 4 percent could entail selling more stock than expected to sustain the income stream and reduce the potential retirement capacity. On the other hand, as you wait for a market rebound, the part of your portfolio that includes high-quality dividend stocks will continue to pay you at the same cost. Although your net worth could be smaller, your revenue stream would remain unchanged (until the markets return). Furthermore, if a dividend is paid, the company cannot stop if circumstances get bad. A non-dividend spent business with a beautiful stock price appreciation will see it dropping just as rapidly if unexpected issues occur.

And how much of your portfolio will you spend on high-yield income stocks? This is a question that can only be resolved. It depends on a wide variety of factors, including your age, the amount of money you are expected to spend, the time you are prepared to invest to ensure that you have a portfolio with high return inventories with the highest quality, particularly your personal risk appetite and your investing style. Honestly, don't believe in a formula to decide what percentage a person would have in any market segment. Believe in conducting your work to ensure that you learn and appreciate the firms you invest in and why they demand better than average returns for high-income shares.

Be comfortable and ensure that the "good night's sleep" test is passed. When you're so concerned about your investments that you can't sleep, you don't spend on your risk appetite. While watching the talking heads on Television, I can testify to many analysts and political experts from all sides of the table. Others say the economy is going up, and others suggest it is going down. Some people are optimistic about the economy, and others fear like we are heading for another slump. For the right blend of high- yield dividend-yielding equities as part of a diversified portfolio that fits your standards and risk appetite, you can be even better positioned to draw in for the future or whatever the future is, irrespective of the direction of stocks and you will depend on a disrupted income stream.

How To Pick Dividend Stocks And When To Buy?

Why does a stock slightly higher than other stocks yield a dividend? There could be many explanations. High profits are also a symbol of high risk. If the risk is actual or expected is a matter to be decided by each investor. Another factor could be the stock type. If it is a Business Development Company, a Master Limited Partnership, or a Real Estate Investment Trust, the high dividend is partly due to government requirements that the vast majority of the earnings be passed on to stockholders to maintain a free corporate tax status.

A high yield may be due to the stock's price falling dramatically due to a general market slowdown, downturns in that particular industry, or unfortunate news for that specific company or shares with similar characteristics. The yield decreases as the price declines, and the dividend remains the same. Again, the real value of the individual stock under review may or may not reflect this. Often that helps in the understanding of the product you are reviewing. Know the company, where it concerns its competition, and how it performs relative to previous quarters or years. You should exclude it from the scanning system, whether you don't know what an organization does or do not appreciate what it does.

Price concern or period: The price of a stock is a very significant element in its choice. Every commodity is up and down, regardless of whether the economy is up or down. Some of these improvements are driven by demand, and very particular steps influence others. Strong returns continue to fluctuate dramatically before and after the ex-dividend period. The crowd that catches distributions needs to get the payout. Many that are interested in capital gains want to purchase and sell before the pre-ex-dividend climb. Many buyers only want to buy before the payout, while others want to buy after the stock declines after the ex-dividend date. The price will also be profoundly influenced as a company purchases new inventories to raise funds.

Because MLPs, BDCs, and REITs tend to make much of their money, they also sell extra inventories to finance new production. This is often viewed as a dilution, and after such an announcement, stock owners often sell this. The aim here is to see whether it is merely a dilution or whether future sales from growth funded by selling new shares would more than outweigh the increase of existing shares. Perhaps the only way to do so is to see what happens before and to see what the company thinks it wants to do with the revenue from stock sales. Knowing the typical price cycle of a stock and its impacts is essential in terms of purchase timing.

Statistical metrics: Take a glance at stock benefit levels to see if a particular asset falls in. When the PE is very high relative to other businesses, it raises a red flag. Likewise, if it's too low compared to equivalent machinery, why? A small PE caused by an irrationally low price is the way to look. Metrics such as book price, purchase rates, cash flow rates should be analyzed in the historical sense of this particular product and within the market in which it operates.

Questions to ask: Is the dividend safe? Is the payout entirely covered by revenue or cash flow? Whose proportion of profits is paid in dividends? It is necessary to know the company's debt to equity ratio in manufacturing companies. Generally speaking, it is easier to have more equity than the debt that yields less than a shareholder liability ratio. Similarly, more existing assets than current liabilities are usually desirable, with the current rate of 2 or higher typically being a reasonable standard. Such formulas do not explicitly illustrate REITs, MLP's, and BDC's, and issues such as the cash flow allocation, hedging, debt, curve of yield and rising interest rates are as significant or even more important consider. Once, comprehension of the business under discussion also matters.

In calculating high returns, an organization's size is less important than its place among its competitors, its past success, and its anticipated results in the future. This is also clear that big, well-established businesses with long-term dividends are likely to be healthier than smaller, younger firms. However, the latest Wall Street crash and other empires' fall show that what can appear dull is not, and what is historically stable will not be safe in the future.

Analysts: Most securities are evaluated by at least one analyst and often by five, four, or more. The opinion is based on moral concepts, scientific analysis, or a mixture of the two. There is also a range of computerized analytical web tools such as MSN Monetary (free) and Value Line (fee) that link a stock metric to an "opinion" formulation. Analyst ratings are impressive because an analyst will often place a stock purchase rate, while another sells the same stock based on the same information. Looking at experts' views gives a valuable context evaluation and provides thought-provoking information, but they are not a replacement for your due diligence and personal appraisal.

Nobody knows what your standards are more than you for purchasing, selling, or holding stocks. Nobody knows better than you about your risk tolerance. No one knows how much more money you have to spend on a single market or resources than you. Although it is insightful to look at analyst reviews, note that they just have views, so your opinion will be as secure as or more durable than your own if you do the reading! Note, nobody cares more than you do about your money!

Why Is The Dividend Investing Popular?

Once upon a time, people rarely traded in bonds. Bonds, bank accounts, and Guaranteed Investment Certificates were high income received, so that the buying of securities was not required. With inflation and interest rates rising and long staying weak, people have been looking for other ways to generate money. The two most common approaches are real estate and dividend rent. Investment of real estate includes the purchase and sale of the property and is not addressed further. Dividend contributions will be discussed in this segment through the acquisition of shares.

When it comes to investing in dividends, there are some essential things to remember: profits are not promised.

Many Canadians are aware that shares and mutual funds are not protected until Canadian deposit insurance is adequate. This is usually the case when bankrupt institutions hold your investments. The same happens to mutual securities as to shares. A business can alter or cancel its dividend payment entirely without much warning. This is usually announced at shareholders' meetings and by press releases. Companies that discard or reduce dividends indeed tend to receive poor advertising from the market, thus discouraging them, but it always happens. When profits are cut, they may change the course of the business. One potential scenario is when a company decides to invest a lot of ongoing cash in a new product, new business line, or other company requiring money to grow it. Instead of paying dividends, the company has now decided to conserve its capital and allow the profits instead to generate capital gains. Secondly, the company does not make as much money as before and can no longer afford dividends. A third scenario includes businesses with a negative shock such as a lawsuit, a policy reform that harms their business, a merger, a takeover, or a natural catastrophe that makes the corporation change its dividend course. Scenarios often occur where dividends rise more than anticipated, such as adding extra profits, a one-time dividend payout from a merger deal, the outcome of a dispute, and improvements in legislation that benefit the corporation and result in a substantial increase in profit. Read the media reports and decipher the current situation to find out what is happening to a company. May or may not keep up with inflation dividends.

This year, multiple businesses will increase dividends. In some cases, people believe it because it has been going on for many years. These changes are intended to keep your dividend income stable as the product price falls, charging more dollars for each share of your stock. Such bigger pay-outs help keep inflation going and encourage your investment to retain its value for a long time. When the share price stagnates and dividend distributions are stable, inflation would not keep pace because you will get the same amount for several years. Inflation would not deteriorate. As the price of goods increases, you will find that your money will buy less and less and will pinch cash. It is particularly relevant if the dividends are your only income stream or if you live on a fixed amount of money. Most senior citizens and individuals with set government coverage are listed as such. To figure out what is happening in this situation, look at your business's dividend payment history and figure out if payment raises are planned. If they are often predictable, but there are some sudden pattern shifts, see what happened to the company at the moment. Such intervals will decide how reliable the stock is and is not effective in the payment of dividends.

Dividend yields are influenced inversely by the price of the stock.

The amount of dividend dollars received at the time of dividend payment divided by the share price gives you a percentage called the "dividend yield." This equation helps you equate this return with other assets, such as bond rates or GIC rates. The output can also be measured over time to see what the production will do. Since the stock price is the equation's denominator, the percentage given to you or the dividend yield will decline as the stock price rises. Conversely, this dividend yield will increase as the stock price fell. That calculation would matter to you whether you invest for guaranteed profits and have shared, or if you want to change portfolios or need a certain amount of theory (money spent) for an option to dividend holding securities. When you bring fresh capital into dividend options, this yield contrasts it with whether you have "cheap" (high yield) or "economic" (low return). Many things affect the inventory price so that this yield will change significantly according to the inventory price at a particular time. The dividend payment would not be very fluctuating unless something unusual occurs- as stated in the previous paragraphs.

How Is The Level Of Interest?

When trading in dividend pay-out securities, interest levels will be closely watched. The higher interest rates, the more probable it is that dividend options are issued because one will buy an option, shares, or other interest-bearing securities. It's like a substitute effect – if one thing becomes very costly and a cheaper version comes, you'll buy the more affordable version. If a dividend stock gives you a 5% income stream and a bond leaves you a 2% income stream, you will probably purchase the dividend stock after weighing risks, costs, and taxes. If the bond then provides you with a 4% income because of increased interest rates, this dividend stock is not attractive. If the relationship instead generates a revenue stream of 6 percent, it will already be a higher return than the stock paying dividends. People will sell the dividend stock before the price falls to approximately 6 percent or a corresponding return after risk, costs, and taxes. Because dividend payment will not adjust too quickly, the only solution to managing markets is to modify the price of the dividend stock in this situation.

Dividend Payment Process And how can you receive such dividends? The traditional method is to open a trading account with a bank or brokerage company. The statement must be such that you can purchase individual stocks. You can buy these products yourself, or anyone will buy them for you. Before setting up the account, make sure you ask questions about costs, account access limitations, and taxes. You will buy shares in each company. You would purchase 100 shares of Bell Canada Enterprises, for instance (the BCE trading symbol). Such investments will cost you an illustration of $50 per share. If you purchase 100 securities, $5,000 plus some stock will be paid. Many accounts do have costs to hold the wallet accessible but ask questions when buying products because such expenses can decrease the sum of money you earn from the entire process. You are entitled to a dividend payment every quarter once the shares are in your name.

The quarter-end date is the quarter-end date of the corporation, not the quarter-end date of the year. When you hold the stock that either the name or name of a mutual account listed with the Corporation, the name of the account owned by the securities would be set to collect the payout until the dividend payment date comes. You would earn the dividend if you bought shares before this date. You will instead see a cash payout for the stock in your portfolio. In some cases, the profits can be reinvested in more stocks rather than cash to ensure that you continue to buy more shares rather than yourself. This approach is useful if you want your inventory to expand. When you choose to invest your profits, you shouldn't do so because securities will be traded regularly to raise revenue, which will create some selling costs and expenses to plan the transactions and receive the best profit. This is difficult to time the business, and it cannot be ignored until you have any experience.

When Do You Not Have To Spend On Dividends?

The answer to this question depends on what your primary reasons for buying

Dividend returns and your risk tolerance are. If you just want money and can get your money by purchasing debt, the latter is a better choice. If you are incredibly risky to lose your capital, and a guaranteed alternative investment falls before you, you can instead purchase the guaranteed alternative. When you like dividend income, and like the capital gain that sometimes comes with it, you may want to retain your dividend balance even if other options are offered to you. When interest rates rise dramatically and you miss your earnings, the whole dividend investing principle can be switched off. If you value real estate and can produce a similar income from real estate against investing in dividends, real estate investment is the route for you because you know more about its functions.

Putting all this together, Investing in dividends should always be considered and everything else in your life, both financially and otherwise. Be mindful of what you want for dividend investing to achieve, your choices, and how confident you feel with each option. You will always recognize the amount of information you have about every opportunity. The more you learn about it, the smarter you are. Treat it as an exercise and gradually wade in for all that can be found before you learn a decent deal about it.

The Best Investing Strategies

All right, you've determined what you intend to achieve with saving, so you know what sort of stocks you want. You have a grip on the potholes that can keep you up, and you learned to assess the product's success. Only one move left: to determine if all this experience is applied to your investments. It is both the simplest and the most robust move.

Think of it as a vehicle buy. You did the research: you contrasted the rates with certain distributors; you reviewed the rates of similar vehicles. We also tested the automotive selling industry to figure out whether and where this model performs well. You have spoken to former clients to see how the salesmen go about here. What's your first bid for the car? How much are you willing to consider for payments? What are the choices in the car that you want? It is time to make some serious decisions.

Rarely black and white is an investing tactic. Investment plans are typically a combination of different choices. My perception has been that my investing opportunities are rising directly as my portfolio develops. The amount of investment approaches in my portfolio is also increasing, also directly. Investment plans will stay flexible, like investment goals, adjust to the various conditions you find yourself, and adjust yourself to any fresh concepts.

A complete set of investment plans is not feasible since they are as unique as the employees. Stories talk about people who use dartboards, astrology, and (I heard) even monkeys to select their investments. For a new buyer, though, you will learn some of the more common (and healthier) strategies people use for investing in their stocks:

• Plan for the decision

• Investment approach

• Purchase and keep the dollar cost estimate. The only reaction in the field of finance is yours.

Recommendations

"Experts" tend to race from the woodworks as people hear that you have started your investing career. In all honesty, a significant amount of suggestions you get would have actual validity. Those thinking to the Organizations with whom they operate are well-positioned than the regular citizen on the street to speak to their internal processes.

TIP:

A suggestion is an input or information provided from specific individuals, often not asked, that might have more insight into the product than you do.

Your friends and family will give you a real insight into a company and its goods and services that you do not know about. For starters, you asked a friend of yours who is an engineer to tell you about his encounters with the investment in the Home Depot. We're writing financial books; if it showed up and presented itself to us, we couldn't put drywall. Nonetheless, following our conversation, you feel a lot happier about my ultimate judgment.

Analysis

An analysis is an ambiguous word that may cover almost everything. To invite people to express their thoughts is to study and submit a sample of the organization's annual report. An analysis is the general public's test, as are evaluations of the stock of the Press. As an implication, it is difficult to provide a clear meaning of "analysis" for could stock and/or buyer.

This does not mean that analysis itself cannot be decided; rather, particular investors ought to decide for themselves whether "research" applies to the kinds of investment decisions they assess.

Any investment choice you make will be reviewed. The degree is up to you, but the period you can make your investment decision extremely familiar is directly linked to the investment quality. Ultimately, by betting on market analysis, you fool yourself. Don't make any mistakes; this form of cheating would cost you cold hard cash.

Purchase and keep

Purchase and sell is a great tactic for every beginner that is equally desirable to buyers of all types of expertise. Buy and keep functions such as these: since the introduction of the capital exchange. The securities sold volume has virtually, without exception, risen. The passive approach buys and keeps, operates under the premise that you can earn a profit if you acquire stock and leave it to stay where it is long enough. If it is 5, 10, or 20 years are unclear, but knowing that your savings are part of a larger goal, you will be very confident of a return until your vision is available, and you should be able to sell your stock.

TIP:

Purchasing and keeping is an investing technique in which an individual buys a stock and leaves it alone. Purchasing and holding typically ensure the earnings are reinvested through future equity transactions.

For a plan for buying and retaining, you would like to buy firms' stock with a long-term opportunity. To do this, consider blue-chip inventories or inventories with strong growth prospects. Prospective owners would actively suggest reinvesting their earnings in potential equity sales rather than receiving earnings. Most companies can allow additional acquisitions without increasing inventory pressures, thus enhancing expenditure.

Only the most ambitious investor is best positioned to make a return by refusing broker fees and by enabling compound interest to work its magic on the original investment or the eventual dividend reinvestments.

Finally, the most significant drawback of the buy-and-keep approach is that it needs to waste an abundance of time studying and pursuing specific projects. The buy-and-hold approach is also called the buy-and-forget regarding the policy. As a prospective buyer, you should be well informed of the size of the business. Instead of having numerous specific transactions, you're expected to do more by extensive analysis on a company and "letting it fly." The broker may dislike you because the overall trades you carry out are dependent on his or her profit, but the banker would appreciate you because you hold those trading commissions in your bank account.

The average cost of dollars

The average cost of dollars is another fantastic investing technique that needs careful consideration by new investors. In the overall dollar bill, you spend a certain sum at a daily interval; for example, you take a certain amount from a paycheck. There is little question over the best or mixed outcome of this expenditure method, and data can be found to support either view. However, the dollar's overall cost will not yield negative outcomes and places people on the table who might not spend otherwise.

One of the main reasons people offer is that they don't have sufficient spare capital to spend in the equity market. If the regular person waited for hundreds of thousands of dollars to spend before they were involved, the US equity market would be a somewhat different location. Individuals with big investments never obtain a lump sum comparable to their portfolio's total value. Instead, these large portfolios were built by making smaller investments regularly.

By the way, an average dollar price is not expected for those who want to buy to achieve better asset values. When you are curious about the amount you are charging for the product because it changes throughout the year, then you should visualize the actual amount you have charged for the product using the annual dollar cost and the actual selling price over the same duration from the following graph. In retrospect (over the previous year), you will obtain a very clear understanding of the prospects for an optimum price through buying the prospective stock utilizing the average dollar rate.

Investment Strategies And Human Behavior

The most common influence of human activity on market prices is likely to be an overreaction. All else being equal, a company's basic values on a fair market should decide the stock price, and a direct partnership will exist between the two. Nonetheless, analyses – and a quick look at CNN's inventory on every given day – indicate that the partnership will not always exist as planned.

Investors frequently respond, sometimes violently, driving rates too far or dropping them too low against their foundations. Therefore, the market is not completely justified in practice, but no financial or company-based consideration can impact. The most probable source of the phenomenon appears to be how investors view and react to shocks or news reports or even acts of specific investors. Such overreaction takes place in the financial market, which contributes to a variety of investing approaches.

Contrarian Tactics

As contrasted with existing 'favorites' or what are often considered prestige and glamor products, the overreaction impact is strongly evident. 'Out of favor' inventories are not bad-quality inventories that aren't appealing to the consumer for any reason. It is interesting, though, is that over time, the 'out of favor' stocks should usually outperform the 'favorites.' And as the "out of fashion" stocks are the "favorites" because of enhanced buying, the effect would be reversed, and the cycle continued cyclically, while only small adjustments to the market fundamental can be made. As such, commodities continue to reverse over time because consumer preferences shift, who has studied the impact of an inventory portfolio for ten years.

Primes paying for high-growth inventories are too costly when 'out-of-favor inventories continue to show improved future profits. This reminiscent of a regression to the average, a mathematical phenomenon under which variables appear to balance and are nothing unique. Over several hundred years, scientists have understood that this form of impact also happens while human activity is involved. What is unique is that the impact was observed inside a limited stock domain.

If a commodity is an "out of favor" or its ratios, indicate a "favored stock."

In What Works on Wall Street, detailed and well-researched results were released, which include: book price (P/BV), the cash flow level (P/CF), and earnings values (P/E). Stocks with the lowest ratios will grow fastest, particularly with positive news shocks, and are therefore the ones to be pursued from this opposite viewpoint, given that they are necessarily nice stocks.

Momentum Strategies

Contrary investing approaches represent the reality that making money in stocks needs either 'out of favor' or securities, above and above the smaller yet stable returns of renowned firms like Microsoft or IBM. That is not the truth, though.

In reality, if you were to infer that theoretically, nobody should purchase through stocks-on the road to attractive stocks – and skip lucrative opportunities. However, the investment valuation requires an average of five years to make a profitable return. However, this is always inappropriate, and analysis demonstrates that the trend regularly drives a vast range of stocks to new heights and that profits can be earned on stocks even quicker than five years. You simply don't purchase securities that are up from their fair price owing to financial or behavioral factors. Such a strategy will be unmistakable and may contribute to a defeat.

The first approach refers to product combinations and utilizes the so-called large stock effect.

The one-week return to the following, where around 10 percent of the market increase on next week's return, might be predicted from this return. Since the trend only occurs with investments, it appears that the pattern of lead/lay is seen, only with specific stocks, and mostly for the short term-i.e. regular and weekly returns. This means large stocks lead to small stocks, hence the term. Of starters, Apple rises significantly, and a few days after, there is a price change among many suppliers of computer devices.

Consequently, the purchasing of second-line stocks - medium caps and small caps - in a market that was assumed to be ready for reclassification at any point in the immediate future and then waiting on the acquisitions will operate very well. Although money may be made from trends alone, I prefer a financially stable portfolio and less susceptible to fluctuations as it travels. In other terms, you are contrary to consumer opinion, where the view of consumers is alone that such securities are inconceivable, not against basic financial determinants and economic fact.

The second approach applies to the fascinating results, which show that the high dynamic stocks – as calculated by their previous six months of income – outperform low dynamic stocks by 8 to 9 percent in the subsequent year. Therefore, purchasing high volatile stocks will be another beneficial way to maximize portfolio earnings.

They control LSV Asset Management and bring many of their work results into action. They prefer to resist preferring costly growth stocks with the momentum suffix. Instead, they use competitive indications, such as enhanced exposure and uncertainty to income reports or alerts, to disclose interest stocks that are only starting to rebound in an upward process. This is not a convenient way to shape a portfolio, time and stock choices are essential, but much like the teachers, when you have an expert programming system, you can consider it much more comfortable!

Earnings Surprise Strategies

The key to shaping a portfolio in terms of volatile stocks is to use objective metrics that show that the stock is starting that period. Also, for a particular programming system, it may be a bit tougher than it looks. When addicted to looking at stock returns over the last six months, though, profit shocks should still be seen as the driving factor of overstock collection.

A shock against the assumptions of observers. When the shock is optimistic but beats the investors' standards, you are more likely to be a future winner. However, it should be recalled that what constitutes a successful, positive income surprise is not always obvious, particularly when evaluating whether income can be sustained or repeated in the future. There's no swallow in a night! Has the business ever changed?

Earnings results may often be negatively influenced by investor assessments of the industry, which contributes to overreactions in the extreme that are another valuable tactic. E.g., in three days, Intel plunged an incredibly disproportionate 20% when it announced better second-quarter incomes in 1995. Those were 4% below investor estimates, which constituted the catalyst for the decline in behavioral terms. A transition became inevitable, while profits continued to increase. During spring 1997, the market price of Intel had almost tripled. Someone who understands the organization should have made money in this case instead of joining the investing crowd.

Hewlett Packard is a common startling illustration, as it also highlights how intense investors respond to press releases. Once, the manipulation of this overreaction contributes to successful investment policy. The company announced in September 1992 that its earnings would be below the analyst's expectations. The price plunged 18 percent by the next day. It was an utterly unreasonable and excessive reaction. Truly speaking, leading to the anticipated drop in profits of a hundred million dollars in the coming year, the company's stock value collapsed by 3.5 billion dollars in 24 hours. Of note-if you have so far followed the momentum of this novel, it is not surprising to learn that the price has recovered in full in three months and then some.

With profound insight into certain forms of behavioral trading deviations, which are the product of his performance, and the perception that a successful trader should not have to gamble continually, Warren Buffet was correct to say: 'Simply glance at the market and see whether anyone has done something dumb on the day you can capitalize on.'

Fusion Policies

Another way to take advantage of overreactions that trigger price fluctuations is to take advantage of certain types of fusion situations. For example, a partnership between Royal Dutch Petroleum and Shell Transport was established in 1907. Both firms have decided to combine their responsibilities at a pace of 60-40%, but remain separate in Holland and England. Throughout the early 1990s, RDP listed mostly in the USA as a member of the S&P500 and Shell-operated in the United Kingdom as part of the FTSE100 (Financial Times Stock Exchange One Hundred Index).

While a fair economy allows for years to pass, the two business pieces will compete at the same, or equivalent, ratio of 60 to 40. Nonetheless, recent research has shown that this is not the case; company stock prices do not reflect this ratio. Alternatively, the real price differential between RDP and Shell varied by about 35% after adjusting to vat, trade costs, and foreign exchange discrepancies.

Human actions are again at work to influence and can be done with a subjective method and working with its most lucrative portion. The approach is maybe long-term, so it may be a perfect form of investing for mutual funds or hedge funds.

Apparent High-Risk Strategies

The clear high-risk approach involves coping with assets that are perceived to involve a rather large role because they can contribute to significant losses. This approach explains that

47

misinformation, lack of understanding of transactions, or business conditions cause investors to assume and overreact.

Effective execution of the plan includes addressing these obstacles and evaluating the expenditure suggested rationally.

Here's one definition of junk bonds. These are high yield bonds with poor credit agency scores, i.e., BB scores or lower problems. The basic premise of this, reinforced by Mike Milken and Drexel Burnham's media reporting in the late 1980s, is that they are incredibly poor and highly dangerous. But is this assumption justified, or is it another situation where investors overreact to the details they receive rather than judge themselves? The truth is, these bonds are already available such that anyone owns them-$ 178.45 billion is reportedly sold during the five years ended in 1996 (source: Securities Data Co.). In reality, these individuals might well have based their deals on some records and studies demonstrating the good output of such bonds under the correct conditions. Notably, the low-grade bonds yield on average 50% greater than high-grade ones, and defaults were not any higher (the Hickman study on 1900-1945), the default rate was only 0.01% from 1945- 1965, and even more convincingly that even though the default rate rose between 0.015% and 0.019% by 1981, the yield premium was 4 percent.

That implied that the probability of a win was twenty times greater than the potential loss in default. Yet, there was no hope of a specific reward in the influenced thought of most investors. Despite the promise of what they think is larger returns elsewhere on the board. As Daniel Kahneman and Amos Twerski's theory of expectations suggests, buyers have remained wary of this possibility in favor of what they consider to be healthier stocks, such as the forthcoming glamorous Microsoft and Yahoo!

Junk links aren't for everybody or especially not for the beginner; to effectively exchange them, they need a strong degree of experience; they need a diversified portfolio. They need to be of decent quality, something many don't yet do. However, this approach reveals that there are several better assets than first appears on close inspection. Human nature, overreaction, overweight the interest of external knowledge such as media speculation and analyst opinion, discourage investors from seriously evaluating distressed bonds or related high-risk assets.

A New Generation Of Policies

Though, as we have shown, over responses may be used for various approaches, it is challenging to quantify them as a causal factor in evaluating market fluctuations. Understanding this will give us a successful plan. Nonetheless, the research council also investigates precisely what causes an overreaction. We know the impact, but what does it have? For example, is this an impact that depends on the economy or a specific investor or both? May we say before we see its results that the conditions that encourage it are in evidence? Attempts to use a formula resulted in inconsistent performance, as ABN AMRO has for their behavior program, which has lost about 27% since its establishment.

We will do a lot of research until we truly grasp how human activity functions in the capital market setting.

There is no question that understanding human behavior will increase our chances of investing in capital. Nevertheless, comportment finance specialists have begun scratching the surface with innovative approaches with a comprehensive approach to the mechanisms involved and the implementation

49

with outcomes. In the next few years, even more successful approaches would potentially materialize. The sector itself, a beginner in the financial environment, is just around fifteen and is only starting to demonstrate interest.

Top Option Investment Strategies

Bullish Balanced Tactics

1)   Long Call: Simply purchase an inventory call option. It offers infinite reward opportunities and reduces the related exposure to the amount charged by the stock option. E.g., imagine you have $1600 and think Google (GOOG) is going to grow in value: assume it is selling at $500 a share, but you only have enough cash to buy three shares. Rather than buying the shares, you plan to buy Google (GOOG) call options. Let's just assume you want to be safe and purchase just money trading options ($500 strike). Now you just have to choose the expiry month (you think the stock will soon rise or it takes a while?) Say that you think that in 1 month, Google (GOOG) will increase its value. You buy September 500 Calls for $16 (you received $1000, and you can acquire one contract (sold in 100 board lots). When Google (GOOG) sells in September at $516, you made a profit. When the call options end, Suppose GOOG sells $550. If you had three securities, you would receive ($550-500)*3 = $150. If you bought Call Options, it would be

{(550-500)-16}*100 = 3400 dollars for your profit.

2)   Put Writing (Short Put): Offer only stock options. This gives you the option premium, while the maximum risk is the strike price less the premium received. Your highest chance situation will arise only if the stock price was $0. An investor should typically have a balanced and positive market outlook for this approach. Say that you are involved in Apple (AAPL) and

assume that it would benefit or remain the same. Put on, Apple (AAPL) will be traded, and you earn the bonus right in exchange for the chance that the stock will reduce its value before the equity options you offer expire. Tell Apple (AAPL) has a $120 contract. To be careful, you may pick a strike price of $6 for the money ($120) and an expiry of 1 month. When you write just one deal, you're going to get $600. You can spend $600 on Google elsewhere while waiting for the deal to expire. You made a return because the Company (AAPL) is priced at (120-6 = $114).

3)   Married Put: By purchasing the product and obtaining a shipment, this technique is applied. Which offers you insurance from a fall in quality because you can always take part in the market exchange upside down? This technique is often referred to as a 'synthetic call.' Let's go to Starbucks (SBUX). The risk/reward profile is quite close to the Long Call. You purchase 100 shares at 25 cents apiece for 2500 bucks and want to cover yourself from a downturn in Starbuck's stock price and get the capital right since you're very cautious. Only claim that you want to cover the stock from a one-month fall. Your purchase puts with a $25 1 month trigger to claim $1 expire. Currently, the only money that can be loosed over the month is the $1 that you charged for while always being upside down, so long as Starbucks (SBUX) trades more than $26 at the expiry, you make a profit.

Bearish-Neutral Tactics

4)   Shot Put: just purchase Put on stock options. Its technique is placed into effect because a company requires a limited stock outlook. Assuming you believe Google (GOOG) is going to increase rates over the coming month. You want to purchase Google options rather than Google (GOOG) because you don't want to lose too much revenue. Google is selling Tell

(GOOG) at $500. You need to be able to fill your place if you decide to cut the stock. Say you've got $1500, you might buy three shares. If you are prudent and buy puts, you will compose $500 for a month to claim $15. One deal (100 shares) you might pay. If you had just condensed the stock, you would profit as much as the stock is smaller, yet you have limitless side threats. Your vulnerability is limited to you with the Google choices (GOOG), although the bonuses can be significant. Think Google (GOOG) would sell at $450 in one month. Lack of stock the profits would be ($500-$ 450) * 3 = $150 because the product was borrowed ($500 + $15-$ 450)

5)   Call Writing: Only compose (sell) enticing choices on a product. This gives you the premium option when your maximum risk is infinite (the stock can expand to infinite, ha). An investor should typically provide a favorable market outlook for this approach. Say you're involved in Apple (AAPL) and think it'll decrease or stay the same in the next month. You will offer Call Options on Apple (AAPL) in exchange for the chance of raising the valuation of the shares for the month. Think Apple (AAPL) sells for $120, so you can be conservative, so pay off the cash buying ($120) shares. You get a bonus of $5.

6)   Short Sells Protected: This technique is applied by shortening the stock and purchasing an invitational right. It helps you from arising in asset values as you will afford to share in the decline in inventory rates. The risk/reward balance is somewhat close to the duration put; this is why it is often classified as a 'synthetic put.' You should shorten 100 shares at $25 a share at $2500 and choose to shield yourself against a spike in market price to acquire calls against Starbucks (SBUX) at the cash level because you are cautious. Only claim that you want to cover the stock from a one-month fall. You purchase calls from Starbucks (SBUX) for $25 and $1 month to expire. So

the best you'll get loosened in the month is the $1 you spent because you will also take an interest in every market price decline. So long so Starbucks (SBUX) sells for under $24, you've profited.

Strategies For Balanced Options:

7)   Short Straddle: Concurrently, a Put and Call contract is published on the same product for the same strike price and the same expiry date. That way, you will gain as long as the market price is very steady. E.g., assume Google (GOOG) is selling at $500, and you believe that will stick on to that price for the coming month: sell Google (GOOG)

$500 for $16 and sell Google (GOOG) $500 for $15, all with expirations of roughly one month. As long as Google's price (GOOG) is selling in the first month ($500 − (15 + 16) = $469) and in the second ($500 + (15 + 16) = $531) you have made a profit.

8)   Short Combination: This technique is close to Short Straddle, where you submit a call and an appeal option, but the distinction is that you use specific strike rates for short combos. This helps you to through your window of productivity even if there is a market shift. Say, for starters, Apple (AAPL) is $120/share sold, so you believe the price should stay relatively steady over the next month, but there are a little more reasons than the Short Straddle Investor: selling Apple (AAPL)

$130 Calls for $2, so selling Apple 110 (AAPL) Calls for $3. They also made a boost when the Apple securities are over (110-3-2 = $105) and below (130 + 3 + 2 = $135). This way, you get a lower pricing price but are more likely to make a profit.

9)   This is the reverse of the short straddle, where the buyer can purchase concurrently at the same strike price and expiry

date, a call option, and an option on the same stock. Investors adopt this technique because they assume that an elevated market price can happen in a product but may not realize which way the product will travel. This technique will be effective while a big awaited investment transaction is being made: buy-back plan, policy package, emerging technologies, profit results, presidential election. Say, for example, that the United States presidential election will occur in the next month, and you want to make a profit. Any stocks shift according to the nominee recipient, and you want to focus on Starbucks (SBUX). Perhaps one individual decides to lift milk prices while the other intends to cut it. You know that would impact the bottom line of Starbucks (SBUX) to enforce the long straddle since you don't know who is going to compete. You purchase calls and bring them on Starbucks (SBUX) at the same strike price at the same month's expiry. The stock would most definitely push drastically in one direction when the decision is revealed. As long as the market travels in one direction, you can benefit more than the value you invested in the option premium.

10) Time spreads (calendar spreads): This technique is enforced by the same amount of transactions or calls on the same stock with different expiry dates but at the same expense. Time spreads usually have a neutral basis but may also be built to be bullish or bearish. For instance, sell $500 Google Call (GOOG) for one month and buy $500 Google Call (GOOG) for six months to expire. When calls with a shorter time to expiration erode in value quicker than long-term calls, you will make a benefit. This functions as the time value portion of a choice value typically erode the shorter it expires. Nevertheless, specific dimensions of the quality of options, such as uncertainty, must be addressed.

Investment Strategy Synopsis

Investment policy in the investment planner culture reflects a little faith. Nothings will bubble passions, fly hands, demand police intervention faster than getting a buyer and a publicity fan into space, and tell them to resolve their differences. The reality is that some of the methods work a couple of days, and even Bernie Madoff worked out how to do one thing all the time, right before he was arrested. Investment plans have two key parts:

1)   which investment will be bought and 2) when it is acquired and sold.

Strategies For Distribution (What To Buy)

Strategic asset class management

Behavior, shares, and cash are known as traditional asset groups. Such types are classified into sub-categories depending on the region, the size of businesses (small-cap, mid-cap, big-cap), and the bond forms (treasuries, high yield, mortgage-backed, etc.). Often real estate, derivatives, and mutual funds are included as new asset groups. Strategic asset class allocation aims to build a portfolio of non-related assets that fit an appropriate risk profile. That allocation then sticks to as the price rises and falls. The portfolio is usually regularly rebalanced to retain each property's ratios, but much of the portfolio is left alone.

Most Growing Arguments in support:

•   Easy to create with mutual funds, which are typically associated with asset groups.

•   Mutual funds offer diversification through skilled investment holding of several securities.

My rebuttal:

•   At the same time, most shared fund managers prefer specific equity markets, rendering the market less broad than it might seem (e.g., oil or financially overweight).

•   Over the last decade, most product commodity groups are strongly associated.

The separation by regional area (U.S. & foreign) or the investment market's business value is no longer a diversified fund. This was a long-term phenomenon that has been evolving and deteriorating over the last 20 years or so. As an obvious illustration, as oil declines from 150 dollars/barrel to 35 dollars/barrel, all energy firms are affected, whether big or small, US-based or Brazilian-based. Nonetheless, an asset class distribution approach can be effectively applied for mutual funds to boost total diversification and incorporate different alternative assets.

Balanced market allocation

The key issue with asset class selection, as mentioned earlier, is that the big share groups are not sufficiently diverse to achieve successful diversification. Based Sector Distribution is being tackled by diversifying through low- relationship sectors (technology, electricity, finance, healthcare, etc.). It's not a novel idea. It diversifies nearly any fund that includes individual securities and will execute the Strategy through either specific stocks or sector-based Exchange Traded Funds (ETFs).

Many Popular Arguments in support:

•   Investment extending through different industries is a far more comfortable option to diversify than to split assets due to its scale or where their headquarters are based.

•   Besides, corporate inventories and ETFs have far smaller costs than mutual funds.

•   The distribution of the business may be reliably managed.

My rebuttal:

• When market selection is applied with a few separate products for each business, major corporate threats are introduced to the portfolio.

Semi-objective opinion:

With the dramatic increase in results over the last 10-20 years, the "this only makes sense" Sector Allocation provides a check. A food inventory and a store of oil would intuitively do better to diversify than a big oil supply and limited energy storage. An active fund manager generally allows sectoral allocations to a specific asset class (e.g., large-cap values). Still, there is no collaboration among the managers if you have many mutual funds.

Tactical Inventory Assignment/Tactical Business Allocation

Both approaches are identical, with the distinction between conventional inventory groups and resource divisions. The aim is to forecast the asset or business sector that would perform well in the immediate term and overweight the portfolio to support this product or industry section. A mathematical model, economic metrics, or (more commonly) an advisor's view or intuition may be used as a guide for deciding what asset type or field to participate in or to remain out of.

Many specific supportive points (some of the dubious accuracy):

• The contractor has a reputation for choosing productive industries.

- If on a down market, debit, cash, or protective industries (e.g., healthcare) is best to be open.

- It's possible to time the demand, but most people are doing it incorrectly.

My Rebuttal:

- Enough advisors are doing different ideas, that some of them are scientifically accurate in their predictions. They have their radio program as this occurs. You rarely know from them unless they're incorrect.

- Unexpected incidents or political interference will render any forecast useless.

- Overweighting and avoiding other industries increases the danger.

Semi-objective opinion:

You have to take some extra danger to substantially dominate the business, which is what this approach does. If appropriately named, this technique will allow immense gains. This will even waste a lot of revenue when someone else earns more. It is possible to make money in almost any setting by choosing the best markets or types of assets at the right moment. I am not convinced, however, that the previous achievement is a reliable indicator of potential achievement, close to flipping a coin and attempting to get "heads."

Strategies For Purchasing And Selling

Purchase and Hold

A mere purchase-and-hold approach suggests that you acquire high-quality investments like securities or a mutual fund and only keep investment up and down before your investing priorities shift or find that the investments are not as valuable as you thought. The explanation is because the stock economy moves up over time, and by carrying cash, you don't want to skip a major day in the economy.

Most Important Supporting Arguments:

•   The bulk of price returns exist in a comparatively few days, and if you lose a day, the profit would be significantly smaller.

•   "Business time" is more critical than "business time."

•   Warren Buffet is a supporter of the buy-and-hold.

My Rebuttal:

•   The absence of the bad days in the economy is much greater than even the most reliable days. However, since no calendar occurs that either delays the better days or ignores the bad days, all cases are ludicrous and use them to describe honesty as claims.

When It Works

Buy-and-hold generates profits as assets grow, and as they decline, they lose income. It operates best on rising markets and thus functions badly on down markets.

Market timing (base on predication)

Market timing is one of the most poorly described concepts in the finance sector. Some analysts deride market forecasting, but they conduct market timing themselves regularly. Broadly described, market timing is a technique focused on forecasted market conditions, which modifies a portfolio. Such adjustments may entail selling and transferring to cash of all portfolios or merely modifying equity and bond ratios due to economic circumstances or planned consumer behavior. The prediction-based market forecasting focuses judgments on the estimation of potential developments by a consultant. Investments that protect against inflation will be introduced if high inflation is expected. When the economic decline is expected, a contractor can switch to a heavier cash role.

Most important supporting arguments:

It is possible to predict which markets are more likely to outperform in the future by utilizing metrics such as inflation, factory utilization, unemployment, etc.

My rebuttal:

•   There is no intervention with economic variables, but unpredictable incidents such as political action or regional wars circumvent the mathematical expectation used for forecasts.

•   Overweighting other industries and disregarding others creates a significant portfolio risk.

When it doesn't work:

This approach relies strongly on the person or mathematical model producing the forecast. When the projections prove correct, this approach is expected to outperform other strategies substantially. Unless the predictions are not right, the reverse is true. Due to the vast number of advisors who create forecasts, a small percentage are right many times in a row, but objectively this does not mean a better likelihood of continuing to be accurate in the future. As described above, most mathematical simulations can be disrupted suddenly by unforeseen news or policy intervention.

Market timing (based on momentum)

Market forecasting incorporates statistical metrics (stock graphs and recent business behavior) to assess if the price is down or rising. These are declining patterns were more people decide to sell than they wish to purchase, and rising movements exist as more people want to buy instead of sell. The action of markets and the trading volume will decide when there is more buying pressure or sales pressure at any particular point. The idea behind the momentum is that if a pattern is formed, it appears to stay in position.

Many common supportive arguments:

• Market fluctuations and trading volumes give clear hints as to whether major international traders purchase or sell stresses.

• Institutional traders will not put or remove whole positions in a single exchange, usually spreading trading over some days or weeks. Consequently, patterns appear to stay in position for some time after they have been formed.

My Rebuttal:

• Many consultants can overpower technological trends (head and neck, cup and handle, shallow birdbath with floating handle).

• Such contractors are dealers for short-term moves. On the other side, patterns are more defined by a higher and lower sequence and should not be particularly complex.

Several essential components are required to run this program.

1)   The pattern approach will not be too early or too late. Assets never pass forward. They normally push quickly and then pause or retire. Assuming that a pattern is formed or stopping too early can trigger pullbacks or corrections to spring in. Too long with so many signs to validate can contribute to a loss of a decent part of the cycle.

2)   Liquid assets need to be made. When the machine asks you to purchase or sell, you must be ready to respond.

3)   The pattern does not always continue if you utilize Moving Averages, charting, or other methods to assess patterns. In other situations, each device breaks down, and the goal is to choose a device that is running in the widest range of situations or breaking down in the narrowest set.

Business Timing (Based On Emotion)

It is not usually planned and intentionally applied by those who claim that they dislike the business moment. Most professionals find themselves to be buy-and-keep buyers but wind up switching to cash when the pressure gets too strong or the economy too terrifying. This usually happens when a major loss is already on the ledger, rendering this a momentum source. The explanation is that even if my assets have already lost value, they will also lose money. The dilemma is that if anxiety or apprehension influences the sales choice, then usually the choice to buy is "feeling great," which almost often comes at a higher price than the sale price.

Many important supporting arguments:

• Not so many individuals consciously promote this approach. However, many individuals use it.

My rebuttal:

• Anything but pointing out that you cannot consider yourself a trader because you switch to cash or change your stock allocation while the market is terrifying, so no one can use that as an excuse to "prove" that all timing schemes are doomed to failure.

When it works

This approach never succeeds, which is why most people purchase while the price is up and sell at a relatively small level. What technique you choose doesn't matter. Just about everything is safer than relying on subjective commitment judgments.

Disclosure

The structured Business Distribution Approach utilizes low-correlated ETFs and competitive market positioning. The goal is to engage in upward trends as far as possible and prevent downward trends as possible. This includes a series of laws that unemotionally decide the decisions. A Fair Market Distribution guarantees inclusion at any point in the hottest developments field and a framework to get out of a business as it starts backward.

Weak points:

When a decreasing path lasts a while, selling decisions can only affect the graph's height. The same refers to patterns and judgments. When the market is unpredictable and bounces wide enough to look like ups and downs, but no follow-up happens, a condition can arise where losses are inflated. It will be a very limited and restricted collection of criteria and other tests to mitigate its problem, but it remains.

Blowing Up The Most Common Investment Strategies

Until we begin our study, we need to try some of the more traditional investing strategies.

1)   Diversify your investments by charging a monthly premium of

$150.00 up to your tour 65. Then you can get $3,000,000 if you're in your 60s (if you live so long). We disagree with this notion for many reasons, but there are big issues with this investing approach. Five, maybe you're not around too long. Tomorrow we might all get struck by a truck. Secondly, you need the $150.00 you spend to develop your own company per month. Three, if you'd rather invest in a company you don't have the power to manage, what about your faith? Four, we never encountered a millionaire (and we operated with many millionaires) who assured me their financial wealth was created through mutual fund diversification. FIve, inflation is going to steal the dollars' worth. You will spend $50,000.00 for a new house in the '70s and the same house would run you $200,000 today. What's worth $3 000,0000 when you're 65?

2)   Buy stocks, keep them, and pray for them every day. The entire premise is founded on nonsense. This whole definition is gambling-based. Playing is not gambling. When the strategy is to search honestly for a strong stock and then gamble on the loss, you would be naive (unless you are the CEO). Such a form of spending can contribute to the uncertainty of the next disaster. In our world, wealthy people make wealth in boom or bust periods. In moments of great economic turbulence, Rockefeller expanded his wealth, land, and business scale exponentially. When people keep their money big, they'll sell the $6,000 entertainment room, tv and sofa for $500.00. If people

have no funds, they can sell them their homes for what they owe and not for what their homes deserve.

3)   Invest in one; we learn that he purchases properties. This theory is stupid too, but citizens use this technique to spend their hard-earned dollars every day. My mates don't believe in a man you meet who may or may not be true. If this man has cornfields and operates a beamer, he might not be lawful. Unless this guy has no business cards, he is not legal. Unless this man uses a Gmail account as his main investment email address, he is certainly not legal. Although this man doesn't have a sponsor, he isn't going to be lawful. It doesn't matter if you go to church with him for 30 years or if someone you meet says that they meet someone who likes him and who will share in him back in the day. Do not trust in others without verifiable financial records that will and should display you publicly.

When we continue digging our path with a little more pressure, we have a fast tip on investing in immobilization: If you want to create deep wealth, just ask everybody to learn what they do and do precisely the opposite of what they are asking you. Many citizens would never be wealthy as they are thoroughly assured that their reasoning is right (and doesn't work). The rest of the ordinary people believe they ought to find life methods better and more comfortable, and they don't risk their money. The wealthy always dream about starting learning expertise, to practice to pay bills more and more. The wealthy realize that the talents pay the bills, and the growing the talents, the more income they gain. The wealthy are actively finding opportunities to raise more and more income to spend more and more.

Rich people have a lot to do with complex and versatile economic activity. The wealthy continue to gorge when they dream about all the heavily discounted commodities they will purchase while the economy fails. How far have inventories of the Bank of America fallen? So much income the wealthy

Americans earned on the recovery. While the ordinary consumer needed to pull his capital out and run for the hills when the Dow Jones index plummeted less and less, the wealthy waited for the market to fall, and they could continue planning their major investments.

Are you conscious of the finance theory of Warren Buffett? Warren tells and would warn everyone who listens, "Be scared when the market is gullible; be gullible when the market is scaring." Why? Why is Warren trying to claim that? She claims this because She is an activist billionaire. He became a self-made millionaire when She became a billionaire. Before becoming a millionaire, he was the college boy who invested his time actively seeking to develop as many investing techniques as possible. Before the college boy, he was a high school boy who had property he leased out to a businessman, who paid him monthly to sue his estate.

 Warren Buffett, a pimple-faced high school grad, reported high school investments than the 50-year-old farmer who rented the property. Warren let the farmer work hard to make profits. Growing month the Farmer mailed Warren's mortgage on his lease charge.

So this query goes to you before we continue. Do you want to be mediocre, or would you want to excel profoundly? Would you like to work in a job that you do not like for the rest of your life to diversify so that you can live on a tight budget or want an abundant life? Want to pay off people's mortgages such as Warren Buffet? And do you prefer someone else to pay down your debt like Warren Buffett did at high school? Were you willing to pursue that and continue doing the odd stuff you have to do to excel with your investment? Do you prefer to drive anytime you go to work, or would you want to live for the remainder of your life for the weekend? When you don't want to learn, just stop reading it. Read on when you are ready to expand to the next level. Yet the quick word of caution. Their suffering is rising.

You Want To Spend Strongly, So What Do I Do?

You're not lonely if you have a deep urge to invest, just don't know what to spend in. They are in the same boat as millions of Americans. It's all right, don't just sit in this boat.

If you are like many new investors, you might want to invest in the big IPOs you've heard about. Or maybe you want to invest in a building for offices. There is, however, a problem here. You can't read this for most of you.

The government won't allow you to invest in many of the best investment deals. Some people don't learn, so if you're a non-accredited buyer, you won't even be willing to indulge in any of the better offers. Why? Why? When you become a qualified investor, the government claims that you would be unable to learn what a successful or poor investment is. If you want more detail, we strongly suggest that you use the 1933 Securities Act exemptions. Here's a brief rundown of what the act means (the state shifts its mind): 1) You're an authorized owner because you reach a net valuation of $1,000,000 or more.

When you receive $200,000 or more over the past five years (or $300,000 together with your spouse), and you have a fair goal of achieving the same amount of income in the next year, you become a registered investor.

My friends, several of the big investments that qualified investors will create need a minimum commitment of $50,000 or more. As stated earlier, the bulk of people who read this would not be willing to invest in the office building or the next big IPO. We will not, therefore, dwell on the financial credentials to become an approved investor. We also must focus on the intellectual skills needed to create sufficient capital to become an approved investor. You need the following funds / personal resources to become an accredited investor:

1)   Schooling-Talents are covering the bills. Anything you would do for which customers are willing to pay?

2)   Practice — You ought to learn the financial terminology. "Knowledge without knowledge is useless." You will be willing to compromise. You must be willing to interact with a branch. You will learn how to locate the best prices. We require expertise. We require knowledge.

3)   More capital than you require - You require more resources just to spend. When you have enough money to fund your Lexus, finance your big house, and manicure your mom, you never have enough time to spend afterward.

And how can you accumulate these materials and specific instruments?

If you decide to gain specific skills, you have to serve in a professional mentorship or internship. Find and work for a wealthy business person even though it implies living without pay. How many people can pay now for higher education? $20,000? $40,000? $50,000? $100,000? Perhaps citizens are willing to pay $20,000 for college, but aren't they able to work with the wealthiest people in America free? This is real. That is true. How did Rockefeller begin? He moved to Cleveland to work as a bookkeeper. The boss agrees to compensate him if he does a great job in his first month of service.

If you want more funds than ever, you have to have full liquidation. You have to get rid of those fees for your vehicle. Rich citizens have no allowance for vehicles. You have to eliminate off all the needless gaming expenditures. Cancel it because you have a TV you don't use. When you buy a $2.00 coffee a day before operating, you will avoid this activity. You're going to need the cash early. You can't win if you don't have any dollars. If you don't have the self-discipline to save capital, the roots of excellence are not inside you, paraphrase effective writer Brian Tracy.

Growth Investing Strategy

Big Goals

Growth Strategies Companies are actively looking to locate the best assets of tomorrow. They look for companies that already show signs of success in the early stages of their growth cycle. When they see the right product, they purchase it, even if the price rises have already been rapidly increased in the hope of handling the boom as the company grows and draws more and more buyers. There are not many analyzes involved in investment in growth; they are criteria-based strategies. If we tell criteria, growth investors are much more worried about whether a business has a history that indicates that it can be a pioneer of tomorrow than regarding the structural or technological dimensions of a share.

The metrics used to pick growth stocks differ considerably; however, in general, Growth Investors search out firms capable of controlling their segments and rising growing profits and sales over the next several years. Many companies deliver a unique advantage, such as a state-of-the-art technological technology (early Microsoft, Bill nearly had the world), a revolutionary entrepreneur (stitched employment at Apple) and a strategic benefit (e-Bay still have competition) and a fresh and groundbreaking approach to marketing (Starbucks: are you offering coffee or a lifestyle?)

Investment selection methods

There are a little fundamental analysis and a technical analysis involved in determining possible stocks for production. Still, most of them aim to determine the competitive position of the stock in the sector. They will not be fearful of weak assets until their growth stock expectations are met. For example, if you have a new technology patent company, you are the first driver of a hot new market, and a manager with various successful startups will purchase it even though it's in debt. Most increasing investors would lose money.

One of the simple ratios that you will learn is the price-to-earnings ratio or P / E ratio. A simple calculation is the equity profit split by the stock price, and because they enjoy the metric, it shows you today how investors expect that the stock will do tomorrow. Whereas other tactics would perceive a high P/E ratio to suggest that a stock is already overvalued, a participant in development interprets this as implying that in the future, it would gain even more and investors were merely betting on potential earnings.

There are no guidelines for recognizing growth stocks, although there are a few basic standards for investing in development that most investors stick to. As we mentioned, a growth business must be a pioneer in a new industry; a growth company requires a sustainable competitive advantage. Patents, emerging technologies, deep wallets, or first-mover advantage may take this type. You should recognize that the P / E ratio is significant, which indicates that increasingly growing earnings are a critical part of the plan. Cost reduction is something that goes hand in hand with fast sales growth. Revenue is high; however, if costs rise higher, profit margins are starting to decline, a typical pitfall for many supposed growth stocks. Eventually, if a stock passes the difficult early stages of a sales process and becomes the obvious winner, it must be handled quite strongly. Development Investors still decide who is in charge. We would want to see members with positive backgrounds, the strongest visionaries in their profession, or modern and creative company models.

This is a little wrong, but have you found that expenditure in development and wealth valuation is essentially counter-strategies? An investor with interest will call a big stock an investor with development found garbage and vice versa. Will that say one approach is right and one approach is wrong? No, both have proved to be industry beaters for investors who successfully apply their strategies over long periods. However, this reinforces our advice not to combine approaches. Can you picture an investor in development and value? Yikes. Yikes.

Risks

Creditors would face much more uncertainty than other businesses and policies. How is it? What does that mean? This ensures that their stocks are lowered first and fall the highest in bare times. Due to their existence, many young firms have large P/E ratios and are deemed overvalued through market crashes and recessions. Development Investors must be willing to fail before the market is optimistic again.

Although growth investing is not as technological or quantitative as a strategy such as value investing, it is also a very research-intensive strategy. Development Investors will be more up to date than only on the sector, recognize growing markets, regional regions, and sectors that are hot and learn emerging innovations, companies, and goods fast. Successful development Investors are increasingly switching to different forms of stocks to ensure that they stay concentrated where there are more competition and creativity. There is a huge amount of research to find out what's "soft" on the market right now. There is a common perspective of any journal, forum, and magazine.

Growth Investors will be willing to filter all this knowledge and identify the stocks that will be the champions of tomorrow.

Risk reduction is a challenging but essential aspect of growth expenditure. Most investments use buy limits and sale limits to stay balanced and help cope with this relentless equilibrium. Properly established purchase limits prohibit them from adding capital to stocks with more of their spikes and asking them when they should take advantage of them. Setting sales caps asks them when to cash out investments gained as much as they can lose the specific purchase. It reduces the chance of bad stocks, though, if you set weak limits as growth investors lose big while their capital is cash during a rally. Growth stocks can surpass the index tremendously through positive times, but not if the capital is on the outskirts.

It is not a buy-and-hold policy, you sell a LOT, and you can easily sum up the trading costs. If the purchase or sale limits fluctuate, a successful risk management system can allow you to buy and sell the same stock repeatedly.

Benefits

Growth stocks rise even quicker than other stocks, and during bull markets, you can beat the price significantly. That is the target; Growth Investors realize that by investing in strong rising stocks in rallies, their big returns would more than account for their losses on bear markets.

Capital spending is most inclined to sell out at the peak of a company's development period, stop buying it before it's too late to step back and sell a product when it appears to no longer act as a growth stock. Significant risk investors should be shielded from risks and still have a lot of their capital invested in stock spikes.

Let's be frank; everyone wishes that Google, Microsoft, or Apple purchased businesses. Growth investing is the approach that offers you the greatest shot at making a household built. This is one of the only approaches that the next-generation engine, which can evolve from a company to a blue-chip, is actively seeking. This reason attracts more consumers than any other to invest in prosperity. Most buyers want to buy companies that make them believe they have won the lottery.

Long-term outlook

Growth investing does not go anywhere; it is a very common approach that still draws many investors searching for big returns in bull markets. Significant Growth Investors would outperform investors with almost any other approach. Both of these approaches are more aggressive and provide slightly more protection against stock market losses, but they cannot afford to boom in bull markets because they cannot handle the risks involved.

One downside from development is that you would have to change strategies when you get close to retirement. As your wealth grows considerably as you reach the end of your career, the maintenance of capital is far more important than capital growth. Why? Why? Imagine, for example, that you are just three years from retirement and recession. Because you are a rising trader, your portfolio declines more than the economy, and you lose 40% of your assets. You have plenty of healing time if you are 15, no problem, but if you are just three, you cannot account for your losses and very unlikely to win further ground until the day of your retirement. You will have to consider if you want to operate later or maintain a lighter schedule after retirement. The lack of choices is no fun; wiser people turn to a more conservative portfolio fund strategy.

Investor Profile

You would perform multiple hours of work a week over the first year or two and find high potential growth stock at an early point of their development process if you chose this strategy. Study history can tell you a great deal about how large companies operated and were seen early on in the sector. Study and job integrity cannot be emphasized sufficiently. The media are too hyped on what markets and sectors are "soft," so good growth investors are willing to skip all of the hysteria, so discover star businesses hiding in the rubble. You will do a lot of diligent work to improve and build the selection criteria.

It would have to have an iron resolve and a heavy stomach as a growth investor because it will face risks in downturn markets, sometimes quite easily. Successful investors embrace this uncertainty as a natural malaise and push it away, hoping for the next recovery to wash away the losses. Risk reduction works; however, keep in mind that risk management for a growth investor relies mainly on time-saving acquisitions and selling of the growth stocks to boost gains than it does on defending you when the demand declines. Typically, as a bear market strikes, you should be completely investing in high-risk securities. You may have to acknowledge certain gross spots. Such quick, often massive losses make it tough for anyone but the best growth investors to escape dumb risks such as panicking and poor profits.

A growth investor aims to recognize the best businesses tomorrow, and often it feels like trying to locate a needle in a haystack. You must eventually select losers, particularly as a novice. The best way to overcome it is to start developing the requirements and risk reduction strategies to select fewer and fewer losers to get rid of them quicker to better.

The purpose of this book is to summarize some main stock market indicators and valuation and to allow investors to make informed decisions in a fairly clear context.

There has been a wealth of information on stock investments, regularly attacked by financial media on buyers. This knowledge stream is distributed through several media channels. Many business tools offer useful information, but such findings cannot support better decision-making. Research has demonstrated that the valuation line will scarcely cope with the stock index despite its highly detailed research. Research has shown that "superior" research and timely implementation is sufficient to resolve the Demand Index. The word used is Alpha, Warren Buffet, George Soros, Peter Lynch, and several more Alpha searching Gurus examples.

Until developing a more holistic stock structure, it is necessary to identify specific stock investment categories. Stocks are usually defined as specific or favored inventories. The biggest distinction between the two is the following. Second, preferred stocks are favored by the owners in case of losses by the firm over common stocks. Second, favored inventories are obtained to produce dividends (income) with less appreciation capacity, whereas specific inventories for dividends and capital appreciation may be used, focusing on the latter. Thirdly, preferred stocks are in some situations like shares, because interest rates continue to raise the desired premium, interest rate variance has a large degree of association with the overall stock market as the equity market gets hit with rising interest rates. With increasing common stock, the impact of interest rate variance would rely on various variables, particularly on the company's capital (or debt) structure.

Certain popular equity groups include First blue-chip stocks of well-known Dow Jones firms with an existing investor dividend policy background. Second, stocks of values are underrated jewels that are expected to rise over the long term. Thirdly, growth stocks are development-oriented securities that are valued higher due to their anticipation of potential appreciation. Fourthly, cyclical inventories are prone to market cycles. Fifth, products that stay stable through market changes like services.

The key indicators of equity trading are listed below:

• Fifty-two weeks High-Small: Check out the commodity values in the equity market and equate the present commodity price to the high and small stock values over the previous 52 weeks. The theory is simple: in growing markets, stocks with lower values have a better opportunity than stocks, which have hit the high point of 52 weeks already.

• Capitalization of the Market: This measure indicates how large the business is. Market capitalization is accomplished by multiplying the sum of the company's issued securities by the current stock price. Inventories are usually categorized as major, medium, and small-cap stocks. Big cap stocks, like Exxon, typically do not have a strong upward pricing range relative to other jewels in the mid-cap and small-cap stocks segment. The previous group of mid-cap and small-cap stocks is more likely to compensate for rising star acquisitions, which normally rise 10-fold over a while.

• Volume: This measure shows us how many dollars a day are being exchanged. Volume is determined by multiplying the amount of traded stocks by the average price on a given day. The holdings of blue chips such as Mobil, Microsoft, and Apple are higher. Small to mid-cap companies, by comparison, have fewer reserves, thereby providing a liquidity effect.

• Income development (past and future): This is a crucial indicator for product demand calculation. Profits per share (EPS) were determined by measuring the company's profits by the number of outstanding securities. Earnings development is significant in two ways (year-by-year YOY): whether earnings have risen over the previous five years; and if the real earnings have surpassed the expected gains in the current year. The resulting rise in profits measures the success of growth firms. The issuing of further options dilutes fascinating earnings per share; or the exchange of fixed income assets into common stocks. This will reduce the EPS amount. When a corporation sells the stock, by comparison, the profit per share will grow proportionately. E.g., if a business buys up half its stock with an excess of cash assets, the EPS will arithmetically increase, rendering it more appealing to shareholders. Recall the EPS is closely associated with the market price. Accordingly, purchasing back stocks and believing the external conditions do not alter will eventually contribute to market price changes.

• Price to income (P / E) ratio: While there are several exceptions in that formula, the P / E formula is the most common in the field of stock investment. The P/E calculation is only the present market price split by 12 months of historical profits (though investors also use even 12 months of expected profit). Development investors expect earnings growth regardless of the course of the stock price. On the other side, the interest buyers like the P/E ratio decrease to search for underrated jewels. Quality investors usually track firms with a growth rate in profits higher than the P/E ratio. The second indicator valued by VAT creditors is that the present P/E ratio is below the average over the last five years.

• Price to Sales (P/S): It is generally accepted that businesses often change accounting processes to maximize revenues. This deception is very complicated to add to the revenue figures. This measure shows how much money you are prepared to spend on the company's produced revenue. This figure will tend to be lower for development businesses. However, in contrast with value investors, growth investors are not serious about this factor. Price buyers prefer the percentage to be smaller.

• Price to book ratios (P/B): The asset value indicates a company's valuation because it was liquidated today. The price to book ratio directly measures the company's stock valuation to the net profit. The biggest concern is that this measure relies on the company's financial properties. Investment analyses have shown that intangible goods do play a very significant function in producing interest for shareholders. That explains why the P / B formula is not a complete metric.

• Creation of interest and development indicators: Many equity investors have been based generally on the EPS (Earnings per share) measures in the last five years. Although profit and disposal are like an enterprise's life bloodline, it can also be dishonest to base stock buying decisions on earnings (and sales). More importantly, the analyzer will carry out a more thorough review of the following three key areas which ultimately decide the company's earnings (sales):

A-The consistency of the company's revenue and the appreciation of revenue's accountability (compliance standards). How are the company's success prospects?

B-Net operating margin or revenue quality: what are the company's plans for reducing expenses and increasing shareholder returns? Management plays a vital function in increasing the size and efficiency of profits.

C-What is the cash flow position? The buying of inventories of companies with positive cash flows is significant.

•   Dividend Yield: This calculation is typically applicable to big businesses like the Dow Jones Industrial average. 9- Dividend Yield: It is less applicable to small and high-growth businesses since they do not pay dividends. Based on their risk tolerance and financial priorities, certain creditors would choose big corporations to produce dividends reliably.

•   Relative Market Strength: This statistic measured asset values in a congruent category last year. A close distinction is made in earnings per share for stock siblings. Investor's Business Daily normally conducts this sort of research.

•   Equity Profit (ROE): This is a significant measure showing how much profits the company earns at its owners' hands. Simply stated, it clarifies how the organization utilizes capital effectively and generates income. This metric is particularly applicable to investors in production. Development businesses will track the Return on Equity (ROE) for maintaining positive net present value (NPV) for development ventures. The ROE measure speaks explicitly to the management's depth and expertise.

•   Investor Stake: The larger scale of the investor stake is usually claimed to reflect a greater measure of the company's performance. It is essential that since investors become partners, they must work tirelessly to move the business forward. However, this measure separately cannot imply a company's power. There may be occasions where owners sell inventories to raise revenue from increasing personal and company needs.

•   Predict on a company's success: A company's worth is not dependent on its past performance. This is because past performance is only relevant to help observers predict future patterns and progress. However, no assurance remains for the external climate to stay the same and for the business to replicate its previous performance. The projection (predictions) of the company's projected profits and sales is often tricky. Investors will conduct their due diligence and determine how real profit and sales targets can be met.

• Integrity and management scope: This could be the most critical indicator for estimating every company's potential success and direction. Performance is a relative term that differs according to the complexity of the product. For example, from the viewpoint of growth companies, success is measured by annual growth (YOY), thus retaining a positive return on equities (ROE). The successful launch of creativity in the form of new product introductions improves their results to technology companies. The warning is that creativity is hard to measure because it falls into both tangible and intangible sectors. E.g., how can you quantify Apple's performance or long-term value? The omnipresent presence of emerging technology renders this job much more difficult. Overall, management depth, experience, and dedication are the most critical indicator for evaluating a company's potential performance.

• Stock volatility: This measure is critical to make decisions about the investor's risk-return profile. Simply put, variability is a function of how much returns vary from the average value in a given time. Higher variance means higher risk. In the short term, uncertainty appears to be higher and smoothest down to a degree over the long run. Volatility, of course, relies on the connection between stock price and market fluctuation (called beta).

The latter concept must be holistically analyzed. Again, when these measures are mixed, valuation, and development, investors are viewed differently.

An interested buyer will rely on the long-term strategic advantage, market recognition, and overall existing valuation.

On the other side, growth buyers should pay about past and future growth patterns, regardless of the company's price volatility for 52 weeks and growth potential.

Dividend Stocks

What's All The Hype About?

The Federal Reserve has reduced interest rates to record low levels to assist the US economy are rebounding. The Fed started its plan to retain low-interest rates until 2014. Classical revenue-producing portfolios, including savings bonds, deposit certificates, and money-market funds, cost virtually zero. Creditors are paid, but savers are disciplined.

Low-interest rates might have boosted the economy slightly, but they have been disastrous for older persons with poor-risk appetite. Investors and their consultants tend at low-profit options, but such cars are inherently in greater danger. Many buyers prefer purchasing stocks that pay stable dividends between these alternatives.

Dividend-paying stock opponents say that dividend-paid firms are weak, and they will spend their cash back into the business to stimulate production. Such critics are evidently in the growth portfolio, where the majority of investment returns are supposed to be produced by capital gains. Dividend-paying equity supporters believe that businesses distribute their gains with customers and commitment.

What significant have long-term dividends been? One research analyzed the components of U.S. portfolio net returns between 1802 and 2002. Dividends paid for 5.8% of 7.9% of the annualized sales during these 200 years.1 Further analysis of the global stocks from 1900 to 2005 showed that real profit in seventeen countries was about 5% when they were dividend yield was 4.5%22.

Studies often demonstrate that companies receiving dividends are much better off down markets than their non-dividends-paid peers. Both the research mentioned earlier papers and several others, depending on the assumption that dividend-paying stocks produce higher total returns and lower volatility rates than non-dividend-paying stocks.

Investors mustn't be necessarily trapped in the pit of purchasing stocks because they have strong dividend yields. The unwary investor may buy financially fragile companies such as banks with dubious value. Many businesses will briefly offer a large dividend to preserve a good picture for their creditors, even if present and projected profits do not sustain paying for dividends. To reduce risk, creditors have to consider corporations' financial ability by a rigorous screening procedure.

Several of my latest analysis ventures has built a portfolio of dividend-paying securities in major financially sound firms with reasonably small dividend yields in response to client demands. As the foundation for our study, we have used two dividend-paying stock portfolios: 1), SPDR Standard & Poors Dividend exchange-traded fund (SDY), and 2), Folio Investments Dividend Yield Folio.

The SPDR S&P Dividend Exchange-traded Fund (ETF) consists of 60 securities and is designed to closely suit the S&P Aristocrats Index's high-yield income yields and apps. In choosing the top 100 firms with the maximum average yield, calculated for market capitalization, Folio Investments developed the Yield Folio using the concept of fundamental investment research.

For the 160 inventories examined, 80 have been through our stringent filtering phase. As a result, the Collection of 80 firms has been aptly known as the "Dividend 80" portfolio. We divided the funds evenly to eighty securities to construct our layout, reflecting 1.25% of each asset portfolio. Over the last ten years, surveys have provided findings to confirm the empirical work we quoted in this report.

An analysis of the Morningstar Principia ® portfolio reveals the Dividend 80 fund has outperformed the S&P 500 over the last one-year, three-year, five-year, and ten-year cycles substantially. Over the last ten years, between 1 March 2008 and 28 February 2009, the S&P 500 suffered the largest twelve-month fall of -

44.85%. Over the same 12 months, the 80 income fund will have declined -33.26 percent.

Another check reveals that the 80 dividend portfolio should have produced a 27.80% return over a brief five-year span from 2/21/2007 to 2/17/2012. The S&P 500 Index with dividends recorded a cumulative return of 4.05 percent in those years, and the SPDR S&P Dividend exchange-trading fund posted a return of 7.41 percent.

We are concerned if some method of investment is becoming too common. When buyers had to hold dividends, their values would rise, and returns would decline. We don't think that the market is even near to that level, but the possibility of such a development is worth our focus.

While dividend-paying stocks do not provide coverage for savings accounts or CDs, they have a significant role to play in a well-allocated investment portfolio as one market. Dividend assets entail heightened market risk, but investors with an investment period of 20 to 30 years will be willing to consider these market risks to combat inflation.

Dividend High Stocks

Despite the latest dividend cuts by traditionally dependable dividend-paying firms, income investors find it more difficult to secure high dividend yields. Indeed, Standard & Poor's predicts 2009 will see the most significant decline in dividend pay-outs since 1942. The market downturn has produced many unintentionally high dividend options when businesses who've preserved their dividend pay-outs instead of share price drops unexpectedly find themselves paying out historically high dividend yields. The other side to this sword is that many businesses are cutting their dividend pay-outs to save cash, believing that their high pay-outs deliver a good yield, despite their high share price.

The increased volatility associated with the market's decline has devalued investors' principal, leaving them with less capital to invest if they choose to re-balance their portfolios.

A valuable, defensive approach that genuinely capitalizes on the market's instability to bring in high dividend yields is the Covered Call Sale or Buy/Write technique. The elevated market uncertainty also raised call option prices, providing buyers the ability to sell high yield covered calls on several options, in turn granting them a one-time "double pay-out," minimizing their original investment cash outlay while thus offering them some downside security. Since no firm will slash the premium on their call options, these instruments are equivalent to an "ironclad" dividend. Yes, the new call premiums are also offering buyers higher returns than the underlying portfolio dividends. Even though the firm does slash the pay-out, the buyer will still keep the premium from his covered call offer. In turn, a call seller earns the call premium money back into his account after payment (usually exchange date plus three days).

A covered call investing also gives you the opportunity for capital gains, in addition to the high dividends that you get from the call premium/dividend rate, should the stock be issued (sold) at expiration. Investors frequently offer covered calls that are roughly 5-20 percent above the stock's market price, allowing themselves to gain an additional 5-20 percent benefit, should these stocks climb above the covered call thresholds before the end of the trading period. Considering the record depths that many businesses' share prices have sunk to, many mainstream value investors believe they are purchasing these stocks at undervalued rates and expect a solid chance of them in the future.

To demonstrate this strategy, let's take a look at the values for NYSE/Euronext (NYX), as of March 4, 2009 trading close: STOCK COST/ SHARE:$16.36 ANNUAL DIVIDEND:$1.20/SHARE DIVIDEND YIELD:7.33 percent CALL STRIKE PRICE:$17.50 CALL PREMIUM:$3.25 STATIC CALL YIELD: 19.86 percent CALL EXPIRATION DATE: JAN. 15, 2010 Overall STATIC YIELD: 27.19 percent TOTAL Future Allocated YIELD: 34.16 percent As you can see from the yields in this example, this stock's 19.86 percent call selling return is 2.7 times its dividend yield of 7.33 percent. Thus, even if they cut their dividend, the buyer would still have about 20% less cover in this case.

The dividend remains intact; overall downside insurance in this contract is 27.19 percent (the sum of dividend and call rates), equal to a net static return. Furthermore, by offering a call at the strike price of $ 17.50, about 7 percent over the $16.36 cost/share, this trader now has the opportunity for an estimated cumulative return of 34.16 percent to make this plan very impressive.

Sample Trade Summary: $11,91 Gross re-selling price: $17,50 Dynamic Renditure: $435,00 Allocated Renditure potential: $559,00 Static Call Reddit: Reddit discovered when the underlying shares are NOT assigned at or before the end of each contract. With the "normal" case, the stock share price does not increase as much or as close to the combined cost of the strike price, plus the call premium, to make it worth the buying on the other side of the trade by the call buyer. In this case, the share price will be higher than or near $20.75 ($17.50 strike rates plus $3.25 call premiums) so that the call investor can use his right to purchase the shares.

Total static return: The dividend return combination and the static call return Allocated Call Yield: yield obtained when ARE assigned the underlying securities at or before expiration. That usually happens if the share price of the stock falls to or exceeds the average price and the call price that allows the securities to be issued (sold) at the strike price, which is $17.50 in the above case.

Risks and limits: there are risks, as with any project. This approach cannot promise that these stocks will no longer decline in value after you have bought them. Nevertheless, this value-based, 'double dividend' call strategy provides more downside protection at least than if the stocks were purchased only, and the call premium reduces your cost base.

Upside Risk: Because the upper end of your profit potential is determined, you should be mindful that even though your stock is well above your price and call premium, you are always forced to sell it at your covered call strike price that reduces your profit potential. It's generally wise to look into the call's theoretical value in an options price model, such as Black-Sholes, before investing in assessing the probability of an appeal resulting in money when it expires. You should always evaluate the stagnant and delegated profits before making your protected order (buy or write) plan. You should always test. Several online brokers have automatic pricing choices that ease this process.

Downside Risk: The most significant risk factor for selling protected telephones is that you spend a lot more money than just buying a call alternative. Research has shown, however, that the chances of selling options favor buyers.

You will ensure that you thoroughly research every stock before applying this or some other technique.

However, as previously noted, if the inventory declines after your breakeven, if you want to maintain your underlying position, you should always be able to "purchasing in" to offset many of the losses.

Investing Sound In The Bear Market Coming

We're on a hunt for wolves. Since last July, the stock market has moved sideways or downwards, and although not 20 percent off last year's highs, just wait. Don't get stuck in a denial state. The proof is glamorous - the fiasco of subprime loans and CDOs, other derivatives with risky equity and debt, bank and finance freeze collapsing immobilization bubble, the tragic depreciation of the dollar, appalling revenue and spending government deficits, panicky federal reserve cuts in interest rates, the collapse of Bear Stearns, state unsuccessful compensation stimulation, bond insurances. You may tell, stagflation? But dramatically lower interest rates did not help.

The world is going in loops. The last significant decline came at the beginning of the 1990s. Leaders of government, banks, the media, creditors are anxious. There is a lack of confidence. The excesses of the late 1990s Internet bubble, the latest immovable bubble, and the proliferation of distressed mortgages that were withdrawn as AAA loans all have to be swept off the grid before normalcy can be regained.

The fact that we will never take Wall Street literally. We spend a couple of chapters analyzing the spectrum of deceptive and inaccurate street guidelines to prevent misleading investors. Some of the most negatively impacted streets are their ever-favorable capital market prejudice. You can't count on the road to warn you of pessimistic viewpoints or high risks. A declining market is characterized as "volatile," which never wishes to articulate negative adjectives. A drop in the market is a "correction," but recovery is never called a "mistake." The stock market failure has lasted for 4 to 6 months, but the distribution of the investment in brokerage research rating is 49 percent.

Brokerage firms earn profits by marketing new and recycled securities and bonds to customers. The conflict of interest. It's a conflict of interest. Why will the goods they choose to sell to consumers ever bearish? Don't expect objective, even cautious advice on the Wall Street bear market. The street does not even acknowledge the contraction. In the Federal Reserve, the policy is the same, and the view is still good. Barron sums up this stance: "All is good, but not to fret; things will get better early." If you hear from Wall Street, the president, the Federal Reserve, or the championing media such as CNBC, all of them say that we will be able to resolve these problems and recover by the end of the second half. Both of them are pie-eyed optimists. This is what you would suspect. Yet we promise you, just wait a few months, Pollyanna's forecasts will continue to fall away and move the rebound until the end of this year, or maybe in early 9. The first bad news is never the last one. This is not a matter about whether the country should fall gently or barely, nor how rough the landing will be. This is the first economic slowdown since 1991-92. It will last as long as home rates are low. Uncertainties over the election year and the next year's bitter medicine with a new administration are not a beautiful picture. Financial institutions will take a long time to lend, with bad news like delinquent credit card debt surfacing. International business revenue is rising. The equity market is already priced on a PE multiple higher than the long-term average, which does not reflect any profit reductions.

Protect your capital Security is paramount, especially in the weakening market now. Capital spending is so expensive to substitute. A 35% decrease in value requires a 54% recovery to be even. The aim is not to lose, to prevent significant losses. The adverse risk of any investment in the portfolio must be measured. Mostly expect the worst. Don't look at Wall Street to report inventories understudy for the lowest demand range. Is it not strange how the analysis reports display upward price goals but rarely the worst price risk? The most crucial risk strategy is likely derivatives like equity options, puts, and calls, despite the leverage. First are different market stocks. Stock index funds are marginally less risky and exchange-traded funds. Diversified mutual funds are also at risk. It's sharing, followed by cash in the scale of threats. Review the investment balance carefully. Be sure to weigh your places at the tight end of the ladder in the coming bear market.

There are reasons for continuing to keep stocks in a portfolio, even in a slowdown. Whether you're like me, you have proper inventories you like to hold for a few years. The selling of these will incur taxes on capital gains, and the trend is never to repurchase them later. And if you follow my advice in Full of Bull, you pay decent dividends that reflect a substantial profit in your financial climate. (Historically, about 41 percent of the average capital market return came from dividends between 1926 and 2006, 59 percent of stock price growth, which is my emphasis on dividend payout money.) When the payers are purchased at cheaper rates, the return is likely to be about 10 percent. You're not going to give that up. The problem is the proportion of stocks in your portfolio in a weak economy overall. They conclude that investors should slash their portfolio weight by 30%-50%, even though it means giving up dividend income for a while. It's just about money protection.

Low-Risk Portfolio Plan In A Business Slump

The future price drop in stock with reasonable PE multiples and high dividend yields becomes more constrained as the bear market becomes apparent. They are certainly not immune to the erosion of the market. Nevertheless, their risk is much lower than the high inventory of products. Corporate income in this situation is a significant support factor. PE doesn't mean a lot of "E" isn't accurate. Income stabilization is an essential base for mild stock price downturns. When the starting point is already reasonable, the PE ratio could decline, but not excessively, say PE 10x to 15x. The inventories to be held in the middle of a growing contraction are assets in which productivity is not cyclical, at least where the income potential is resistant to current conditions, such as pipelines, storage, and transportation. By the way, such a portfolio is also a sound investment in bull markets.

The other remarkable asset is the dividend yield. It is a symbol of financial stability, good cash flow, and good quality. There is a direct positive association between dividend payout ratios and income growth. This is an incredible friendship. The higher the salary, the greater the payoff rate. This is unlikely that a $20 stock offering a 0,80 dividend, a 4 percent return, would slip below $10, i.e., an 8 percent return if the sales and the cash flow remain positive. The worst case is around $12, 6%-7% of the dividend yield, if stable, offers an efficient safety net. So an investor should consider seriously buying more shares at this distressing stage.

Consider Other Defensive Techniques.

Gold is, in my opinion, a good bet in the present uncertain financial landscape. Gold provides a safe harbor during a recession or a highly uncertain economic time. The falling economy, the condition of financial institutions, and inflation all point to gold as a tool for protecting the capital's worth. Exchange-traded funds (ETFs) are a particularly simple way of buying gold as an asset. They are a classic game, and they follow the gold price rigorously, are traded regularly, and are listed on major exchanges. A drawback of gold-related ETFs is that dividends are treated as collectible at a rate of 28% instead of the 15% long-term capital gains tax on asset appreciation.

Limited inventories are another protective mechanism after a significant stock decline. It, though, is more speculative and would thus only constitute a small portion of the investment portfolio. Betting that a stock will decrease will lead to endless losses since commodities can grow forever but only fall to zero. Timing, uncertainty, and even the supply of shares to lend are challenges. Identify the areas of business that the slowdown or other market cross-cuts will severely impact. Check for the neediest firms. Then pick inventories with valuations that still have enough contracting space. The method is daunting because stocks most vulnerable to the risks ahead, such as in-home housing, banking and trading, and consumer shopping markets are apparent and have already crashed. You will be on the front and have a balanced perspective. Cut your losses as shares shift in the opposite direction and rise by 10 percent in the event of a shortfall. The risk is so pronounced, it is a tight leash. However, shortening is a way of offsetting declines in your long-term, high-quality, value-added dividend-paid investments.

Allow And Be Happy For The Marketing Bear.

The most challenging part of keeping the financial portfolio ready to cope with a significant equity market collapse is to realize the horrific circumstances and the declining stock market and that things are much worse. The investing dimension is more comfortable to decide the correct, costly stock positions to produce capital. A significant goal is to build a pile of cash or liquid counterparts like a traditional capital exchange fund to enjoy most business tanks. Bear markets are tricky, behaving in a way that hides the downward trend. Every when a steep decline happens, there is a moderate recovery. There are two steps down and one step up to keep you fooled and offer false hope. When bear markets have been commonly established, it's all too late. Bear markets are going in waves, and everyone gets injured in the process. But it wasn't yet this excruciating point. Right now is the only time for the investments to be updated and adjusted for the future bear market.

Characteristics Of Good Dividend Stocks

The right income stocks have simple characteristics to recognize. The attributes allow you to evaluate the predictive dimensions of your investment firm. The statistics are stable and increase every year. Whether the figures remain stable across the years, they always remain a strong business. Also, if there are one or two years in the five or ten years, it's always worth saving in dividends or supports you in developing your financial liberty. Now that you know that accuracy is the main thing, let's look at the different apps.

1)   Dividend Yield – a financial calculation that indicates how much a business charges from the purchase amount (the

amount you buy the asset), in dividends, per year. Despite the absence of capital income, the return on a portfolio's expenditure is the dividend yield. Payout gain is measured as a total payout separated by the paying share amount.

The annual dividend is due for $0.50. Then the dividend return is 5 percent. Two separate income distributions have to be taken into consideration. The first is to utilize the 12-month distributions. You take the last twelve dividends split by the share price and get the gain. Once you launch your study, you will know your desired yield. The bigger the payout, the greater. It allows you to maintain your financial independence by producing more taxable profits from dividends. Please note that returns fluctuate all the time as market values rising and decrease. The bonus sum can even adjust for better or worse. Please note each time you plan to invest in testing these details.

2)   Sales or revenue-it's a clear reality; there is no money for purchases, no benefit for earnings. Therefore, dividends cannot be charged without benefit. As an investor, you will ensure if your company's revenues are through. The higher the revenue growth levels, the higher the savings because that can contribute to more gains that will be taken back of your financial independence because of dividends. Before investing, please test the sales pattern of your prospective firm.

3)   Profit-also referred to as profits or EPS. Profit allows businesses to expand, contributing to more dividends. Higher revenues are equivalent to safer businesses. The healthier the business, the more likely it is to increase its dividends. Higher distributions have greater yields on investments. You would now get sufficient capital to recycle the profits to meet strategic and passive salaries. Several metrics of calculating productivity are

available; the simplest is the return on equity (ROE), the higher, the more reliable.

4)   Debt-the money owed by a corporation. The bigger the leverage is, of course, the easier it is for dividend income holders, as the corporation would have enough capital to compensate you. Too much debt may be a concern for potential payments of dividends. The corporation will experience tough challenges and a drop in earnings, reducing the sum of dividends charged. The corporation may need the funds to cover obligations and does not have enough to fund the dividend. The debt-to-equity ratio (D / E) lets you and the lender easily see if the debt is too heavy.

5)   High Free Cash Flow Margins - Cash management is all about business. The firm can not organically expand its enterprise without healthy cash flow and can not pay dividends.

Your spare cash to businesses. Healthy businesses will translate a significant proportion of their revenue into free cash flow, contributing to higher dividends. Good dividends and their reinvestment would allow passive income and independence to fund.

6)   The regular dividend per equity is the low distribution amount, separated by profits per share. The smaller the dividend payment ratio, and the greater the income yield, at least 5 percent, the stronger the investment rate. The larger the distribution level, the greater the probability that the dividend would be that. For starters, businesses that spend 80% of their dividend profits per year may have to cut their dividends if the company goes down. That is why you will always look for companies that expand or at least don't decrease in revenue. A small dividend payment ratio, therefore, helps the income to rise.

Investing in businesses with marginally above-average dividend returns but with substantial potential for dividend appreciation over time is ideal for income seekers with long-term planning, as it can allow you to obtain further dividends. This brings you more passive income. You may use or reinvest the dividends to rise and reduce your income to reach your financial independence.

You may assume that everybody thinks just for the stock prices they buy. Who's going to risk money? Okay, if the economy is down, income investors matter even less. Dividends are the greatest supporter of creditors in the capital market. Dividends are quietly helping you develop your financial independence and deferred profits. Dividends are not attractive enough to gain publicity. We are not 'the big hot venture' because we are not producing millions in the short term. It is accurate that other businesses that pay for dividends do not survive the slump in the economy. Financial firms, in particular, were struck hard.

Nevertheless, it is necessary to note that saving dividends is the safest and most straightforward investment approach, consistently producing the highest average return. Dividends in your wallet are money. You don't have to offer a stake to earn dividends. The bulk of dividend plans are ongoing. Companies with proven systems never slash their dividends or cancel them. They are closely tracked and recorded, making it simple to collect details. When trends of dividends have been developed, adjustments are announced instantly. Over time you can move from a paycheck from a hard job to a dividend paycheck, which gives you financial independence anytime you choose, not because you have to.

Strategies In Investing In Dividend Stocks

The main aim of buyers when trading in securities is to gain a split profit. If that is intended to fund expenses, compensation for entertainment activities, or merely recycle, customers like to learn wherever their capital goes. Whenever buyers purchase securities, they earn a percentage of the company's profits if the equity price rises. That part, which a shareholder earns from his or her equity assets, is considered a dividend stock and is usually paid out to allow buyers to purchase more business equities. Because various investment approaches exist, these techniques must be taken into account.

Why Trade-In Portfolios With Dividends:

Data stock

When investing in securities, the first significant thing to remember is that the firm charges dividends or not. It will be achieved because not all assets are restored to dividends. Many businesses require you to invest in securities but don't offer a dividend. An individual should check the Wall Street Journal to decide whether or not a stock offers dividends. Also, the investor should register for an electronic account to track dividend-paying stocks.

Company selection

The main hazard to income stock will not compensate. Corporate variety If a corporation is considered a tenuous cash balance, it would typically have no equity distributions to carry out periodically or annually. Investors are smart to search for businesses that will meet their fees quarterly. Suppose a corporation can't afford its expenses. In that case, that ensures that it cannot compensate its shareholders' dividends, a business that also increases the payout and will not slash income is a perfect investment for you.

Company's perspective on dividends

While it is not appropriate for evaluating a business based on its previous operations, its experience in paying dividends may be advantageous. When you analyze a company's history and recognize that it pays dividends reliably, many dividends will be gained from participating in that business.

Healthy income yield

Another technique to consider in the hunt for income stocks to invest in is the business's dividend yield. The profit of a business is defined as the total sum reflected in stock at the present price. In plain words, the dividend yield applies to how much income you get on your dividend payment. A dividend yield that is deemed safe meets or reaches 3 percent.

Try investing in dividend stocks approaches and consider what you aim to achieve: preserved dividend stock earnings.

Why Dividend Stocks Make Great Investments

In 1934, the traditional term "Protection analyzed the company's primary purpose is to pay dividends to its investors." It was popular to assume that the likelihood of stock price appreciation was uncertain; therefore, the shareholdings' justification was the continuous influx of dividends.

Yet 66 years later, several buyers have virtually little leverage in dividends at the close of the 18-year bull market from 1982 to 2000. The unprecedented surge in equity values over the long term raising the allocation of dividends to net returns. No one will sincerely claim that the primary aim of the shareholding was to earn dividends.

As we all know, this bull was a bubble, and over the three years, the bubble burst between 2000 and 2002. As the dam gave way, it destroyed thousands of people's financial savings and sobered other creditors.

There has been a revived valuation of dividends and dividend-paying securities since 2002. Investors know that a dividend share fund will reduce the risk, expand gradually, and increase sales slowly over time.

You will potentially get both production and profits with strong dividend-paying stocks. Dividends are the hidden asset of stocks. Research suggests that dividends compensated for about half or more of the overall capital market gain over a long time.

This may shock you, considering how low commercial dividends are. No commonly publicized dividend index receives coverage on the Dow, S&P 500 and NASDAQ indices daily.

Yet all such indices just represent shifts in rates. As a consequence, they offer a somewhat imperfect image of "how stocks are performing." It is no surprise why dividends slip under the radar of many buyers.

The typical misunderstandings are that dividend shares are

- Slow-growing and boring;

- A sign that a business cannot think otherwise about money; and

- Perfect just for families requiring income.

Such definitions are completely false. In reality, dividend-paying stocks are appealing to someone of any age as a key investment.

Yes, dividend stocks may only be the most significant choice someone may possess. Seven explanations for this:

1.   Dividend inventories have a decent net gain. Notice that overall return is the main objective, not just price appreciation. Net return = value for capital

+ dividends.

2.   Dividends are charged moderately. The official statutory government income tax rate is 15%.

3.   Practices with distributions continue to endure. Dividend paid businesses are typically large and well-established. The majorities of them never slash and lift their dividends. Dividend raises also arrive at a far quicker rate than other consumers would have. (See below # 5.)

4.   You don't have to sell the securities to collect the payout. It's all given to you. You should do something about it: preserve money, reinvest it, or waste it. (Look at #7 below.)

5.   Dividend levels will rise with time as compared to bonds. So the right securities with dividends do that. According to Morningstar, S&P 500 companies have raised their dividends annually by a total of 17 percent over the last three years. Neither loan does because the central bank does not.

6.   However, unlike shares, because the principal is invested in securities, it can over time. Bonds are "set" investments: you earn back your original expenditure towards the conclusion of the debt period in dollars devastated by inflation. On the other side, stocks have traditionally been the only asset class above inflation.

7.   With your returns, you can do anything you want. Such dollars are not "trapped" inside portfolio holding. You will recycle them if you are young, even in the same business, to develop your wealth more rapidly. It calls into action the "miracle of compounding." When you are a disabled citizen, you will use the dollars on a monthly salary. Or someone would do something for them: re-invest some and spend the others etc. It's thrilling, satisfying, and enjoyable to get dividend shares. In both ages and periods in existence, some people will be prudent to invest heavily in dividend-paying securities.

Using Dividend Stock Screener

It's not easy to pick a dividend stock to invest in, which is why screeners are accessible to you with various parameters such that you can identify the particular form of stock you want to invest in. This is important to keep in mind that securities you invest in will help you meet your financial objectives, revenue targets, and life goals. Using a portfolio screener, you will locate the dividend shares that suit your needs. Most blogs and brokerages sell you dividend screeners with their requirements. The stock or volume ratio, gross margin, PEG levels, dividend yields, and market capitalization will be checked at the dividend securities.

There are also dividend stock screeners that allow users to look at dividend growth in recent years. Using these choices, you can conveniently and rapidly draw up a shortlist of businesses that match your needs. If the category of stocks is established, you can invest in the screener and have a forum for reviewing all the listed firms. You have to closely analyze the underlying considerations, such as whether short-term or long-term influences influence the stock. Looking at the dividend past, you can even have a clear idea of how the distribution is handled. There you need to find businesses that consistently raise their payouts, especially if you have a frequent growth in dividends.

Income stocks give investors a minimum cash flow source that provides reliable and large income returns. The dividend yield is also regarded as the dividend price ratio on every company's shares. The dividend payments are taxable distributions, or a business calculates the dividend price per equity split up by the market value. Dividends-based securities were found to be most valuable when used as a reliable source of profits. The dividend stock screener to select from should list all companies that set up dividend shares in which to invest. This screener will also be easy to use and quickly browse across different stocks.

Since all of these screeners exist, it is interesting to look at any of the various screening places and see the reviews from past screener users. Often ensure that the criteria are well-sorted to render finding the correct screener simple.

Top Dividend Stocks To Buy Now

2 Most buyers worldwide are searching for the right securities to purchase in these difficult financial times. This is especially relevant for recent purchases in the summer of 2011 with the imminent debt crisis in Europe. It seems like another major financial crash is a slim possibility if Greece and Italy don't get back on track. Nonetheless, for certain factors, this period is distinct from 2008, and the US banks are much more capitalized today. We do not expect a potential slowdown or financial crisis and think the economy's recent downturn would be a perfect opportunity to allocate high-income stocks to your investment portfolio.

Many people do not realize how good interest in stable dividend stocks can be, which offer big returns year after year. For starters, between 1970 and 2005, dividend-paid stocks produced an average annual return of more than 10 percent. This is six percent higher than unpaid inventories registered in the same era. What essential is another six percent over 25 years annualized? You'd have produced enough to be a millionaire instead of $200,000 with an original expenditure of $50,000. Therefore, investing in any of our suggested dividend stock picks could deliver high dividends as well as double-digit development for the next five or six years. This could produce an annualized return of more than 20 percent.

Our opinion is that investors must have quality stocks that regularly pay cash dividends, particularly when there are current market volatility and a long recovery period. This is also a safe financial policy in prosperous and bad times. Over the last decade, everybody seems to have overlooked dividends securities, but dividends remain the most significant way to earn money over securities in the long term.

While evaluating good dividend securities, we consider utilizing some significant main parameters. The first is that the business has a ratio of profits (PE) < 14. The traditional average demand is 15, and the current PE rate is 17. The PE level would then be willing to revert to the normal or recent average and still get the demand upside down. The second goal is to demonstrate consistent progress over time with high annual incomes. The third is a major bonus because last year, the business consistently raised the dividend. There are a variety of other conditions for businesses that are valued at < 2.0 (historical average 1.94) and have a Product Revenue Ratio < 1.0 (historical average 0.86). A few other parameters are also helpful.

We concentrated on discovering a diversified collection of 10 really large dividend shares ideal for this book's retirement portfolio. Such businesses are inherently stable, and for years to come, can have strong sales and steady growth.

10 Top Income Stocks to be Buy with Interest, Steady Development, and Reliable Dividends:

1)   BBL - BHP Billiton (PE < 11)

2)   BMS - Bemis Co Inc (PE < 12)

3)   COP - Conoco Phillips (PE < 8)

4)   DD - E.I. du Pont de Nemours and Co. (PE < 10)

5)   EMR - Emerson Electric Co (PE < 12)

6)   MT - Arcelor Mittal (PE < 6)

7)   NSC - Norfolk Southern Corp (PE < 11)

8)   PEG - Public Service Ent Group (PE < 13)

9)   UL - Unilever (PE < 13)

10)   UTX - United Technologies Corp (PE < 12)

Their estimated worth is the upside of at least 20 percent in 1 year. Research these firms and their finances to know how to locate these kinds of assets independently.

In the end, an investor would do well both today and in the future by investing in a top dividend stock. Continue to read some of our reports on strong stocks to be bought in Brazil, China, and elsewhere.

Monthly Dividend Stocks

Monthly dividend securities are investments that every month of the year pay a dividend. If you're still an investor in dividends (or income), you realize that most dividend payout stocks payback to their shareholders every three months or every three months and that such monthly dividend stocks are likely to be fresh to you. (There are also taxable dividend-paying inventories).

As a key feature of monthly dividend stocks, they are typically owned by businesses, trust firms, REITs, restricted partnerships or closed-end trusts in an income-generating fund and trading as individual stocks on daily stock markets (i.e., you may use the online discount broker to purchase them and sell them). It varies from other quarterly dividend paid stocks, which typically (but not always) are specific firms, monthly dividend stocks.

Since several monthly dividends generate profits from various outlets, they have relied on the diversification of revenue streams which can render their monthly cash dividend payments less volatile than individual business.

as a perfect illustration of the danger, and in February 2009, it reduced its dividend by 68 percent. This is a very clear example of a business which is deemed one of the most financially stable in the country, which is commonly owned, tracked by multiple experts, which then cut its dividend, even when one year before it was reduced, most people assumed it should hold its cash payout to investors annually.

When you are an investment buyer in a monthly portfolio, make sure you analyze what securities, bonds, or other properties generating income potentially generate for your chosen stock. When your stocks are concentrated in one sector, such as oil producers, and oil prices are reduced in that situation, your dividend payout (and the price of your monthly dividend stock) may decline per the oil price.

One form of monthly dividend store deserves a special cautionary note for investors who find regular dividends in their portfolios. Although such inventories have a regular dividend profit tax, Canada's rules have been updated and applicable in 2011. In practice, the rules on such transactions have been modified such that they are regulated in Canada as normal companies (now not charging tax) starting in 2011. Such additional income taxes would lower the profits on these assets as part of taxpayers' money as an annual allowance of dividends must also be charged to the Federal government for these new taxes. Please be mindful that the Canadian government excludes 15 percent of these cash dividend distributions to US citizens as a non-resident withholding tax. However, US citizens may still qualify for a partial refund.

As you can see, monthly dividend inventories may be part of people who want dividend accumulation and a constant stream of profits. Still, as always, before buying into these inventories, you have to do your research.

What Is A Dividend?

Dividends are payouts or cash on the profits of the firm. The distributions are business income paid by owners. They pay for a limited proportion of overall income and are typically compensated in money. As already stated, most businesses pay dividends quarterly, while some pay yearly, but you just have to identify the ones who pay the monthly dividends. You will measure the dividends at a set or variable cost, based on the form of stock you have invested in. Remember that businesses are not required to compensate for production. Nevertheless, they compensate the chosen shareholders periodically without the financial turmoil in the business.

Where to Find the Monthly Stocks with Dividends

There are ways to scan for stocks receiving dividends. The central newspaper should be accessed. Local newspapers detail the numerous firms that sell products, or you can search for weekly market alerts in national newspapers. You may use the online source; websites are built exclusively to show the related market stocks.

Reasons For Owning Monthly Dividend Stocks

Monthly dividend shares may allow a return-on-year investor to smooth out the capital (actually over a calendar quarter) over the year. As monthly dividend securities are somewhat different from most shares you buy, there are three explanations for why monthly stocks of dividends can be an excellent addition to your revenue portfolio.

The first explanation of why monthly dividends securities are perhaps the most logical option for your equity portfolio is because dividends are received monthly rather than quarterly. Many dividend-paying shares pay their dividends annually and yield unequal sales over a calendar year. An owner has securities that pay more dividends for a month in a year than the other two months in the quarter. By holding securities that pay their dividends regularly, an investor in equity will get a steadier source of profits.

The second explanation for buying securities that produce monthly profits is that they mainly comprise portfolio firms, closed funds, and royalty trusts. This wealth usually involves a range of income-generating securities, including shares, dividend-paying options, land wealth trusts, and other revenue-generating properties. The positive thing about these kinds of securities is that they diversify through their holdings. You can get a balanced earnings portfolio if you select the right monthly dividend stocks.

The third explanation for bringing the monthly dividend inventory into account is the asset class's options and availability. Although specific inventories include products from several business sectors, a percentage emphasis on those markets enables income investors to diversify their investments under their sector concentration. These inventories have ample regular capacity for an individual to join or leave specific inventories when the time has come.

Monthly distribution options have several income-investor advantages. As always, before you purchase some volume, do your research.

Lightning Source UK Ltd.
Milton Keynes UK
UKHW020647300421
382892UK00001B/64